"MUCH OF WH[...]
SEEM MIRACUL[...]
BELIEVE. CERT[...]
OVER THE YEARS HIS UNCANNY RESULTS,
OBTAINED IMMEDIATELY, HAVE OFTEN
BEEN DIFFICULT FOR ME TO COMPRE-
HEND. EVEN THOUGH AS A DOCTOR I
HAVE WATCHED THEM WITH MY OWN
EYES AND CHECKED THE PEOPLE BEFORE
AND AFTER THEY RECEIVED THE EN-
ERGY, MY DOGMATIC TRAINING MADE
THESE CHANGES IN BODY FUNCTION
AND CONDITION SEEM IMPOSSIBLE . . .
HOWEVER, I HAVE OBSERVED CASES AND
RESULTS YEAR AFTER YEAR, AND I CAN
COME TO ONLY ONE CONCLUSION: THAT
HE WAS BORN TO HEAL."

*from the Introduction by Dena L. Smith, M.D.*

**BORN TO HEAL**

*Ruth Montgomery's story of the amazing Mr. A and the startlingly effective power he taps to achieve his "miraculous" cures.*

# Ruth Montgomery
# Born To Heal

Introduction by Dena L. Smith, M.D.

The astonishing story of Mr. A and the
ancient art of healing with life energies.

FAWCETT CREST • NEW YORK

*this book is dedicated to the whole
of humanity in the hope that all
may gain from the Ancient Wisdom*

A Fawcett Crest Book
Published by Ballantine Books
Copyright © 1973 by Ruth Montgomery and
Dena L. Smith, MD

ISBN 0-449-21111-8

This edition published by arrangement with
Coward, McCann & Geoghegan, Inc.

Manufactured in the United States of America

First Fawcett Popular Library Printing: March 1976
First Ballantine Books Edition: May 1985
Fifth Printing: June 1987

Wherever real names and identities are used in this book, permission has been granted to do so. A few have withheld their names for personal reasons, and owing to the great expanse of years, it has been impossible to trace some of those whose cases are described in the earlier part of Mr. A's life. Thus, fictitious names have been assigned to them, since there is no desire to invade anyone's privacy, although their case histories are in the files. Because some of the attorneys involved in the medical trial of Mr. A are no longer living, I have also refrained from using real names in that chapter, but the transcript is a matter of court record. Except in those instances above referred to, all other names and identities are authentic, unless I have specifically stated otherwise.

Any inquiries concerning Mr. A should be addressed to Life Energies Research Foundation, Suite 406, 3808 Riverside Drive, Burbank, California 91505.

RUTH MONTGOMERY

# CONTENTS

# Introduction

by Dena L. Smith, MD

I feel compelled to introduce the story of Mr. A in order to bring forward the knowledge of life energies, their effects on our lives and health, and to give an indication of what may be accomplished through life energy research for mankind.

I first met Mr. A sixteen years ago when I was a premed student. At that time I had a heart ailment, which he immediately corrected with the energy that he generates—a form of treatment that was totally new to me.

The amazing results he obtained fascinated me and prompted me to study his work. In the hope that I might be able to help people in a similar or related way, I started my formal medical education. I was graduated from the University of Southern California School of Medicine in 1962, completed internship at Los Angeles County General Hospital in 1963, and took surgical specialty training at Kaiser Foundation Hospital in San Francisco from 1963 through 1967, serving as Chief Resident in Surgery from 1966 to 1967. In 1968 I was certified by the American Board of Surgery. In the same year I was granted the Certificate of the Medical Council of Canada and, in 1969, the Certificate of the Commonwealth of England. Despite all of this training, however, it was not possible for me to do what Mr. A does, and I am still not sure that I fully understand his wisdom in healing.

Throughout my years of medical training, I kept an eye on this remarkable man. More and more I realized that the results he obtained in his matter-of-fact and unassuming way were astonishing. He seemed to understand and sense the ailments and problems of people as they walked toward him, or as soon as he placed his hand on them. With this manner of physical contact, he was able to generate human energy to match their individual wavelengths and frequencies, and to correct their ailments in a matter of minutes.

Much of what he has done may seem miraculous, and difficult for many readers to believe. Certainly it was for me at one time. Over the years his uncanny results, obtained immediately, have often been difficult for me to comprehend. Even though as a doctor I had watched them with my own eyes and checked the people before and after they received the energy, my dogmatic training that certain conditions were uncorrectable made these changes in body function and condition seem impossible.

Always a cheerful, kind, and humble man, Mr. A was patient and willing to explain in detail the many facets and frequencies controlling the body. Life itself! Often his explanations would stagger my thinking but would later prove to be true.

Questioning everything, I have not been the easiest to convince. However, I have observed cases and results year after year, and I can come to only one conclusion: that he was born to heal. I feel that his knowledge and use of life energies should be opened to the world, for the sake of humanity. The possibilities of what can be accomplished with life energies, combined with some of our present medical methods, are endless. What I have seen him do for patients before and after surgery is unbelievable. This represents an entirely new phase of treatment. But Mr. A says it is simply the Ancient Wisdom of generating human energy to match each person's energy frequency—as individual as the fingerprints—each person being an individual planet within himself.

Some twenty-five years ago Mr. A published a little book (now out of print) called *Know Your Magnetic Field*, in which he explained some of the fundamentals of life energies. At that time, many felt that the book was written years too soon to be understood; but many of his expressions, unheard of then, are in common usage today, as medical science has advanced. This story of Mr. A is now presented at a time when all of us are eager to learn and understand natural ways of obtaining and maintaining maximum health and contentment.

During the past decade I have worked closely with Mr. A, keeping detailed records of many of his cases and subjecting them to intensive scrutiny. I have observed at first hand his work with thousands of persons suffering from a wide variety of ailments which run the gamut of medical literature, and I have yet to find an instance when the patient was not substantially benefited or healed. Mr. A's explanation of the ancient art of healing with life energies can, in my opinion, prove so beneficial to mankind that I feel that a vital contribution to medical knowledge can be made through his work.

# Foreword

This is an age of seeming miracles. Manmade satellites circle the earth and streak through outer space to report back on other planets. Men walk on the moon, and drive mechanical buggies across its rugged terrain. Communication is instantaneous to any quarter of the globe, and in our own living rooms we watch current events unfold from around the world on television screens.

Medical advances are equally fantastic. A malfunctioning heart is replaced by one which only a few minutes before was beating in the chest of another. Kidney transplants are becoming commonplace. Artificial hip joints replace those badly crippled by arthritis, although mankind continues to be beset by painful ailments.

This is an age when churches and other spiritually oriented organizations are increasingly seeking to revive the Biblical "laying on of hands." We hear of instantaneous cures, cures that are variously called spiritual healing, prayer healing, or faith healing. Books have been written about the healing ministry of Kathryn Kuhlman in Pittsburgh, of Oral Roberts in Tulsa, and of Ambrose (now deceased) and Olga Worrall in Baltimore.

Throughout history, scientific men have scoffed at such "miracles" as the healing waters of Lourdes and other demonstrations of miraculous power which they do not yet understand. Unfortunately, the American Medical Association seems to take the position that a healing is not legitimate unless the person effecting it has a medical diploma to hang on his office wall. Does that piece of parchment itself have magical powers?

This book is about a different kind of healer. He has no medical diploma, nor does he correct ailments simply by calling on God to "heal this man." He works by recharging and revitalizing what he calls the human magnetic field, or master brain, which distributes energy to all parts and functions of the body. Laying his ear to a patient's chest, he occasionally says aloud, "Oh, I've got the signal." As he listens, the vibrations have revealed to him the body tensions and the location of nerve centers which are in spasm. Then, by placing his fingers on certain areas, he generates the particular energy which blends with the individual's, and the correction is usually effected within a matter of minutes. To him it is as natural as for another to switch his radio or television dial from one wavelength or channel to another, seeking the program that suits him best.

Each of us comes into this life with varying talents, which we develop to greater or lesser degree. Just as some have tone-perfect voices, and others a flair for painting, writing, cooking, homemaking, or bookkeeping, so a talent like this man's is not open to everyone. I asked whether his method could be taught to others, and he replied, "Many people have a strong

14

energy current for healing that can be further developed. All that is required is that a person be strong in his own energy, as many are, while others from birth have a weak nervous system. Those with a strong system generate enough energy current to maintain their own needs and radiate a surplus. This is the individual best fitted to heal others, and who could be taught to direct the energy through his or her hands, feeding nerves and releasing spasms, but only in those having energy frequencies complementary to each other. Otherwise, an energy short may result. A baby born under tension has a weak magnetic field, but these pelvic tensions can be released shortly after birth by a person of the properly blended energy who is able to convey the energy to the infant's controlling field."

In *A Search for the Truth* I included a chapter called "The Ancient Wisdom," which told of the seemingly miraculous healings performed by this man, whom I called Mr. A to protect his privacy. In it, I wrote: "We accept without argument the influence of the moon on the tides, because scientists tell us that it is true. We do not dispute the revolving planets and changing seasons in relation to the sun. We have no reason to doubt that a magnetic electrical field governs planetary action. Why, then, is it so strange that a magnetic electrical field might govern human action as well? We are composed of innumerable atoms, and scientists report that the atom with its electrons has the same pattern as the sun and planets in a solar system."

Mr. A—who says that each of us is an individual planet—is a jovial, likable man, rather tall and massively built, with twinkling blue eyes and a ready smile. He does not stand out in a crowd, although in private conversation the forcefulness of his personality is dramatically apparent. When in whimsical mood, he treats his uncanny ability almost as if it were a joke nature has played on him. Obviously Mr. A, who has made a comfortable living in more orthodox fields, including the machinist trade, must sometimes wonder about this strange gift, with the resulting pressures it evokes from the ailing and infirm.

Mr. A totally follows his inner guidance by forces he calls "the Power of Powers." As a consequence, conversation with him can sometimes be disconcerting. Ask his opinion on something and he is apt to reply, "I don't know." Then, a few moments later he may break into the middle of another's sentence to say, "Wait, I'm getting a flash." We pause while he seems to listen within. Then he elaborates on the subject, giving a thorough and often brilliant explanation of fundamentals we had overlooked.

In this book, Mr. A's theories and methods will be discussed at length and illustrated by many case histories of those who have been helped or healed by his ministrations. Since there seems to be a distinct plan to his life, it is possible that Mr. A's years of training in machinery and electronics were essential to his life's work as a healer, because he views the body as an intricate machine which can function perfectly only with proper tuning, oiling, and energy. The life-force, he says, is of electrical energy, and our bodies are mechanically constructed to conduct and transmit the human energy current.

Mr. A says, for example, that a stroke has its origin in the magnetic field. But he emphasizes that it could be avoided by previously releasing the spasm that has built up in the magnetic field, through feeding human energy current to the proper area. He makes it sound as simple as repairing an electric line, although electricity to me is also among the mysteries of life.

This so-called miracle healer explains arthritis in similarly mechanistic terms. He maintains that the magnetic field is the distributor of energy to all the motor points or organs of the body and that calcium is normally circulated throughout our bodies in liquid form, "but any time the field fails to distribute the required energy to keep it liquefied, it solidifies in the weakest sections, such as joints, and at points of sluggish nerves." Mr. A calls this "plating," or "rusting." He says that the nerves, in contact with this solidified calcium, develop pain and irritation, and as the deposit builds up, the joints become frozen and immobile.

As he begins to treat these patients, sending the energy to the hardened calcium areas, the deposits begin to soften and crumble, so that they can be manipulated; and as the energy increases, the waste is gradually eliminated through the kidneys and bladder. This can cause temporary discomfort, but in practically all cases the pain from arthritic joints is relieved within minutes, and as the treatments continue, the swelling begins to subside and then to disappear. The "magic" is the energy generated through Mr. A from "the Powers."

As recently as the seventeenth century, Galileo was tried by the Inquisition in Rome and forced to spend the last eight years of his life under house arrest for declaring that the earth revolves around the sun and is not, therefore, the center of the universe. Nowadays we smile at the ignorance of Galileo's prosecutors and at those who insisted that the world was flat. But is it perhaps equally unenlightened for people of our age to regard as mere superstition the idea that we, like the tides, can be affected by the pull of the moon and the influence of the stars on our human energy fields? Or that by listening, we can achieve inner-knowing?

I believe that the time is not far off when we will accept as a matter of course Mr. A's explanation of an individual's magnetic field, and the source of his healing knowledge. Certainly there are many thousands of healthy, contented people living today who can testify to the healing power generated by this man. "There is no such thing as a miracle," he stoutly insists. "What seems so results from the correct application of natural laws: A miracle is simply what one does not yet understand."

RUTH MONTGOMERY

# CHAPTER I

# The Drama of Healing

For the first fifteen years of her life Patricia Lucille Golden was a Golden Girl indeed. Blond, blue-eyed, and unusually intelligent, she was widely traveled and completely bilingual in English and Spanish. On her mother's side she was the great grandchild of Dr. José Maria Castro, founder of the Republic of Costa Rica, and her father, William Golden, was a consultant to numerous Latin American governments on aviation and oil. Patricia was born by Caesarean section in Powell, Wyoming, on September 23, 1949, but by the time she was six months old, she had lived briefly in eleven states and several foreign countries, before her parents settled for several years in Argentina.

She was a happy, normal, healthy child and was nearly ten years old when her family returned permanently to the United States. There she enrolled first in St. Christopher's Catholic Grammar School in Houston, and later was graduated from St. Cecilia's, after which she attended Houston's St. Agnes Catholic High School—a well-adjusted, extremely athletic girl.

At the end of her sophomore year she began complaining of headaches, and as time passed she became so rebellious, anti-social, and unmanageable that her parents took her to several doctors, including a spe-

19

cialist in neurology and psychiatrists, none of whom were successful in adjusting her to her surroundings. At nineteen she left home and went to California, where she became so ill that she finally checked into a hospital in San Jose. Her parents suffered anguish at her bedside while tests of every kind were run, with negative results, from October 16 until November 7, 1968, after which a tumor was discovered at the base of her brain.

"By this time," says William Golden of Houston, "Patricia was already so paralyzed and nearly blind that it was impossible for her to get out of bed. The doctors stated that an operation would have to be performed immediately but that they saw very little possibility of success, due to the location of the tumor. I was frantic! Fortunately, both Patricia and I had read a book called *A Search for the Truth* in which author Ruth Montgomery told of a remarkable healer called Mr. A. I immediately tried to contact her by telephone, and succeeded in doing so. She told me that Mr. A was still anonymous, but after many entreaties on my part she promised that as soon as humanly possible after the operation, she would arrange for Mr. A to treat Patricia."

I well remember that telephone call from a desperate, brokenhearted stranger whose beloved daughter was said to be facing almost certain death. As gently as I could, I explained that it would be impossible for Mr. A to barge into the San Jose hospital and take over a case which was being handled by some of the finest doctors and surgeons on the West Coast; but he was so insistent, so beseeching, that I finally promised to do everything in my power to arrange for Mr. A to see Patricia after she left the hospital.

Now Mr. Golden again takes up the narrative: "The only reason I wanted to contact Mr. A was that Patricia's doctors had frankly told me the situation appeared hopeless and that it was doubtful if she could survive the operation. After I talked to Ruth Montgomery the operation was performed, and Patricia's medical reports show that the tumor was one of the most malignant types known to exist. They said that it ran down into the spinal column, making it impossible to remove all of the stem. When Patricia returned home to Houston she was in the most horrible condition one could imagine, looking like a victim of a concentration camp and weighing only seventy-five pounds. The girl seemed more dead than alive. Her color was green, her knees were bigger than her wasted thighs, her stomach was concave, her eyes were glazed, and she could not even hold a teaspoon of ginger ale or water on her stomach."

Before continuing with Mr. Golden's sworn statement, which is also signed by his wife, Hilda, let me review what was happening elsewhere. In early December of 1968 my husband and I were at our beach house in Virginia Beach, Virginia, when the telephone rang. It was Mr. A, announcing that he had flown down from Washington because he had heard about my recently broken shoulder and arm and would be glad to see what the energies could do in dispelling the shock of my fall. He must have thought me astonishingly ungrateful, because instead of thanking him I practically wailed, "But you're supposed to be in California! I've given my promise that you will treat a young girl there as soon as she's released from the hospital."

Accompanied by Dr. Dena L. Smith, Mr. A came to our house from the airport, and after I told them what little I knew of the case of Patricia Golden, I secured his promise to do what he could for Pat after she left the hospital. The plane on which he and Dena were returning to their homes in California was scheduled to make one stop in Dallas, and I suggested that Mr. A call Mr. Golden in Houston, from the Dallas airport, to make sure Patricia was still alive, and if so to ask where she would be in California after her hospitalization ended. I subsequently learned from Dr. Dena Smith, who was making an investigatory trip with him, that as the plane circled for a landing in Dallas, Mr. A suddenly said, "We'd better arrange to have our luggage put off here. I've just had a flash that the girl is back in Houston."

Now we continue with Mr. Golden's report: "My wife flew back from California with Patricia, arriving [in Houston] at three o'clock in the morning of December 5, 1968. Arrangements had been made by the San Jose hospital for her to be transferred immediately from the plane to the M. D. Anderson Hospital in Houston, but when Pat said she knew that she would die unless she could come home, the ambulance was canceled.

"As if in answer to prayer, Mr. A arrived with Dr. Dena Smith in Houston that same day at 2 P.M., and he treated Patricia for approximately half an hour, sending what he calls the energies through her lower abdominal area—the magnetic field. After that first treatment Patricia was able to get out of bed and walk with very little difficulty. At six o'clock Mr. A returned and gave her another treatment, after which Pat, who had been unable even to keep water on her stomach, ate a full meal. He had told her to take a teaspoon of whiskey and a soda cracker every hour, and at 10 P.M. he treated her again, although since the first treatment her skin had resumed its normal color, her eyes were clear, and her speech coherent. The following morning Mr. A gave her another treatment, after which Patricia developed a ravenous appetite, being able to eat all that she wanted without any after-effects. At noon, he gave her a final treatment and then said she would have no further problems as long as she lived a normal life.

"Three weeks later Patricia was driving her car again and appeared perfectly normal in every respect, a fact that could not be accepted by the medical doctors of M. D. Anderson Hospital, which is the cancer hospital in the Houston Medical Center and one of the most advanced in the world. Her weight was back to one hundred and fourteen pounds, and her health perfect. It will be easy for anyone to verify this information, and also the fact that no other individual has survived a seven-and-a-half-hour brain operation in her condition, and absolutely no one has survived more than a few months after having this type of malignant tumor removed."

At the time that Mr. Golden wrote this report, two and a half years afterward, he stated, "Patricia is now employed by Texas Instruments, is considered a superior employee, and has advanced very rapidly in her position in the company. There are no longer any behavior problems, which we now realize had been caused by the tumor's pressure on her brain. She has become a very wonderful person, an excellent daughter and wife, and everyone is fond of her, including top management of Texas Instruments. I was having terrible financial problems at the time Mr. A came to help Patricia, but I would have been willing to sign a bank note or anything else he required. He refused everything, and all I could do was pay for his overnight motel bill and airline tickets from Houston. It will never be possible to compensate Mr. A for everything he has done for us, although there is nothing within our power we would not do for him. We know he saved our daughter's life, and more than that, he gave her the strength and courage and desire to do something with her life, and this she is accomplishing in a most efficient manner."

Attached to Mr. Golden's statement was the hospital's lengthy medical statement on Patricia, which reads in part: "A pneumoencephalogram done on November 7, 1968, revealed a large tumor mass in the floor of the fourth ventricle. Through a suboccipital craniotomy a walnut size fourth ventricular ependymoma was removed on November 11. This large soft gray tumor was well encapsulated, extending into the lateral recesses of the fourth ventricle from its point of attachment at the calamus scriptorius, and extending into the more caudal cerebral aqueduct. At the time of removal a visual and auditory representation of relief of her uncommunicating hydrocephalus was appreciated with a sudden gush of fluid indicating her cerebral aqueduct had become unblocked. On histological examination this tumor proved to be a malignant ependymoma. Dr. Lucien Rubinstein, Stanford Professor of Neuropathology, was impressed with the cellularity, the mitoses, the areas of necrosis enough to classify this tumor as a more malignant ependymoma. Dr. John Hanbery, Stanford Professor of Neurosurgery, agreed that the patient's entire craniospinal axis should be irradiated postoperatively, despite the fact all visible tumor was removed."

On receiving Mr. Golden's unsolicited letter, I was deeply thankful for the miraculous healing which the Powers had seemingly effected through Mr. A, but I made no attempt to follow up on the case since I was busily writing another book and now living in Mexico. Much later, after deciding to begin this book, I contacted the Goldens by mail, and in April of 1972 received a joyous letter from Patricia, praising Mr. A and stating, "My health is perfect. Had a complete checkup last Monday and will be sending you a written doctor's report as soon as it is ready."

The report from her doctor in Houston was not long in coming. His letter, written on official stationary, reads in part, "Pat first came to me for care some six months ago, at which time she had been taking Prednisone, 55 mg. every other day. This is a relatively high dose and she had become concerned lest she might have other tissue effects related to that. She had a brain tumor, an ependymoma of the fourth ventricle, resected in California in 1968. Thereafter she had chemotherapy at the M. D. Anderson Hospital, developed total loss of her scalp hair, and went through other debility. She felt that she had had a healing [from Mr. A] before going to the Anderson hospital, but the physicians there continued to keep her on the Prednisone. She first consulted me in September 1971, because she wanted to quit the Prednisone. Other than a fat, puffy face as a side effect of Prednisone, I found no neurologic abnormality at that time and agreed to take her off the Prednisone. Since then I have followed her regularly, and done careful neurologic examinations. She shows no signs of recurrence and is in good physical health." This very sensible-sounding physician kindly gave me permission to use his name, but rather than expose him to possible criticism from his medical colleagues, I am refraining from doing so.

But how typical it is of many other doctors to close their eyes and ears to a healing effected by other means than those employed in their own profession, and therefore to keep treating such a patient with medication. Apparently Patricia's only remaining medical problem had been the unfortunate side effects from needless medication.

Before completing this book, I telephoned Mr. Golden for a check on Patricia. He said she now enjoys radiant health, is a design service technician working closely with engineers at Texas Instruments, and is happily married to Patrick Murphy, a successful young silk-screener with an advertising agency in Houston. When he mentioned that Patricia's aunt and uncle are highly regarded, internationally recognized medical doctors, I asked what they thought of Patricia's unorthodox healing.

"Like any other doctors, they are astounded," Mr. Golden replied. "But having seen Patricia's before-and-after medical reports, and knowing her as they do, they accept the incontrovertible fact that Mr. A saved her life."

I also talked long distance with Patricia Golden Murphy, to verify all facts and understand her viewpoint. She said she had intuitively known that if she went into another hospital on returning to Houston, it would have meant "certain death," and that her only salvation was to go to her parents' home. The doctors in San Jose had insisted she check in immediately with the M. D. Anderson Hospital, and after Mr. A's treatments revived her, she asked him whether she should do so. She remembers his reply: "This is a decision you will have to make on your own."

"I reluctantly went to the hospital after Mr. A left," she continued, "and the doctors put me on cortisone and cobalt treatments, although I felt they were not needed. Finally I refused to take the cobalt anymore, and I wanted to discontinue the cortisone [Prednisone], but by then Patrick and I were married and he insisted that I take it. Then I began having dreams that I was poisoning myself. I therefore located another doctor in Houston, in September 1971, who found no neurologic problem and agreed to take me off cortisone. Today I'm in perfect health, and I'm determined to find my proper role and fulfill whatever mission I have in life."

Through a strange series of coincidences, Pat Golden Murphy is alive and well. Had Mr. A not called on me unexpectedly that day in Virginia Beach, she would have missed the opportunity for his ministrations. He would have returned to California while she was going home to Houston. Had a "flash" not told him she was then in Texas, he would have proceeded with his flight. If Pat herself had not balked at going to the Houston hospital, Mr. A could not have come in on her case at the crucial moment. And had her father not read about the remarkable healing powers of this strangely gifted man, it seems doubtful she would be alive today. Those of us who believe in God can only conclude that He intended Patricia to have another chance, and that her life was saved for a purpose.

Mr. A is the first to admit that not all his cases have been unqualified successes. Often this is because his patients, after one or two treatments, experience immediate relief, and some of them consequently fail to return. Although he knows that without further application of the energy they will not progress, he does not pursue anyone, nor does he pretend to diagnose or indicate the severity of their ailments. The people who come to him must make their own decision about returning, and sometimes their decision seems abysmally wrong. One such case, of which I have personal knowledge, is illuminating.

Shortly after publication of *A Search for the Truth*, a stranger in a nearby state telephoned me in Washington, D.C., with an urgent plea that Mr. A treat her little son, who had been diagnosed as a victim of spastic cerebral palsy. At that time, although more than two years old and able to talk, little Larry could not sit up alone or even turn himself over. I explained that Mr. A was still anonymous, but the image of this helpless child troubled me, and when Mrs. Andrews' mother added her plea, I asked Mr. A if he would see the child the next time he came to Washington.

I was not there during that visit and have consequently not met the family I am calling Andrews, but in November, 1969, I received a letter from the mother, which said, "I took my son to Washington on Friday and Mr. A gave him a total of six treatments that day and the next. After the first treatment my mother and I returned to our hotel room, where I put Larry down on the floor. He went down on all fours and promptly crawled a foot or two. This, perhaps, does not seem far until you remember that Larry is nearly two and a half years old and has never in his life moved alone on all fours. Needless to say, both my mother and I were shocked at the sight.

"After the second treatment by Mr. A, Larry crawled to a chair, pulled himself erect and let go with both hands, holding his back straight, and sat back on his haunches. You can imagine the thrill we experienced at seeing this child, who had never been able to sit up unaided, do such a thing completely on his own. We did not coax him, nor did we aid him in any way. Larry himself was so thrilled he kept laughing and saying, 'Watch this, mom,' and proceeded to amaze us more each minute. We are back home now, and his spectacular actions are continuing in front of my husband and father and neighbors, who are completely at a loss for words. Mr. A says that Larry had a locked pelvis from birth, and that the energy unlocked it. I don't pretend to understand what Mr. A did to my son. I only know that in the last three days I have seen Larry do things he never did before. I can never adequately express my gratitude."

During Mrs. Andrews' visit Mr. A told her that it might be wise to bring Larry in, the next time he was in Washington. A few months later the mother was notified that Mr. A was returning, and would be glad to continue treating Larry, but they did not come, and Mrs. Andrews made no further attempt to communicate.

Nearly three years passed before I decided to write a book about Mr. A and his phenomenal healing powers. Recalling Mrs. Andrews' enthusiasm, I wrote to ask about Larry's progress, and she promptly replied in April, 1972, giving me permission to use her real name and identification, which I am not doing for reasons that will become apparent. Describing in glowing terms the visit she and her mother paid to Mr. A, she said, "Larry had never been able to move properly and, at that point, could not even turn over on the floor, let alone crawl or stand. Mr. A had me undress Larry and lay him on the bed. He then placed his right hand on Larry's lower abdomen, at the same time talking to my mother and myself, and a pulsating motion began in his upper arm and seemed to travel down his arm to Larry. He continued this for approximately five minutes, then told us to take Larry back to our hotel room and he would call us. We returned to our room to relax, and after a few minutes we began to realize that Larry was acting very strangely indeed. We literally could not believe our eyes when he turned over and got up on his hands and knees. He had never done this in his life, and we were dumbfounded. Mr. A called us back from our hotel room several more times and each time did exactly the same thing. And after each visit Larry's behavior became more astounding.

"We stayed overnight, and by the next day he was actually crawling on the floor. He also began to pull himself up to sitting position and then turn himself around by hitching his bottom in a circle. He crawled over to a chair and got up on his knees and then would let go of the chair and hold his balance for a few seconds. While all this was going on, even his personality underwent a change. He kept telling us to watch what he was going to do, and was so talkative! During dinner and breakfast in the hotel dining room he carried on a conversation with the waiter, giving his own order, and he sat in a booster chair, saying he didn't need a high chair anymore.

"After almost three years, my mother and I are still at a loss to explain what we saw. Neither of us is gullible, and I must admit that when we made the trip to Washington we were both very skeptical of the outcome. But even after we returned home, Larry continued to do some of these things. Most remarkable of all, to me, Mr. A refused my offer of payment, and when I later sent him a check he wrote me a letter saying that he would not cash it, and he has never done so. This destroys the question of his being a profiteer.

"Sometime later Mr. A got in touch with me and asked if I wanted to bring Larry to Washington again, but I was simply unable to afford to make the trip at that time. I have often contemplated writing and asking for another appointment, because although Larry progressed well for a while, he seems now to have reached a plateau. My mother and I were subjected to much ridicule when we told what we had seen, even

31

from our families, but both of us remain convinced that he is a great man with a rare and valuable gift."

Thrilled at the progress of this little tyke and grieved at the thought that lack of money should deny him his chance in life, I immediately telephoned Mr. A long distance from Mexico to California, and on learning that he and Dr. Smith were then in Washington, I called there to ask if Mr. A would again treat Larry without charge. He readily assented, and Dena telephoned that same evening to Mrs. Andrews at her home in the nearby state, asking if she would like to bring Larry without charge for a second series of treatments.

The next day Dena wrote me that Mrs. Andrews "hemmed and hawed and said she wasn't sure if she could, or not." Finally she told Dena, "My husband doesn't believe in this sort of thing, and after all, I have to live with him."

But does she? Should a mother, herself convinced of the miraculous power of the energies transmitted through Mr. A, let the narrow prejudices of the man with whom she lives interfere with the right of her child to health and happiness? It is little Larry, trapped in a defective body since birth, who must pay the price of his parents' decision. If each of us is indeed an individual planet, how sad that Larry is denied the privilege of perfect function.

A failure on Mr. A's part? Hardly!

Fortunately, most of the cases Mr. A has dealt with have had far happier endings. Dorothy Hughes of Hayward, California, recently told me that in 1952, at the age of forty-four, she underwent an abdominal hysterectomy for endometriosis, for which a spinal anesthetic was administered.

"Immediately after surgery," she says, "I was aware of excruciating pain in the back of my neck and head, and was very nauseated. I was constantly vomiting, and was aware that my neck was uncontrollably turned to the left side. When I finally recovered from the surgery I went back to work as bookkeeper for the Los Angeles *Examiner*, but I had to wear a neck brace to keep my head centered, so that I could see the pages I was working on, because the distortion of my neck was increasingly severe. Without such a brace, I had to hold my head with my hand to a centered position, from the forty-five degree angle which it automatically assumed.

"Meanwhile I was consulting doctor after doctor, twenty-nine in all, searching for some relief. For days at a time I was hospitalized for cervical traction on my neck, and I received deep neck injections by a neurosurgeon, to no avail. Then I underwent another operation for the repair of a hernia which developed in the hysterectomy scar, which doctors said was the result of my incessant vomiting following the original surgery. Because of my physical condition, the paper told me my services would no longer be needed and gave me my severance pay. I returned to my mother's home in Kansas City, more or less resigned to a life of deformity.

"About a month later, while in church, an inner voice told me to go back to California, and although I could not imagine why, I took the El Capitan train, and was sitting in the dome car with my head twisted to the left, when a nice-appearing man asked if he could share my seat. I said, 'Yes, but please excuse the way I look and the way I must sit.' He replied, 'I'm going to tell you something you may think is very strange, but my wife and two of her friends are going to a man in San Francisco who has really helped them. One of my wife's friends had not been able to swallow food for more than three months, but after one treatment from this man she ate a complete meal and hasn't stopped eating and enjoying her food since. You may think this is witchcraft, but they think he can do anything.'

"I confessed I had been having strange promptings lately that I should go to San Francisco, although I didn't know a soul there, and the man told me how to reach Mr. A. In June of 1953, exactly one year after the first surgery, I arrived at his office, where a large crowd of people waited to see him. When it was my turn, Mr. A listened to my chest and began immediately to tell me all about myself, explaining different situations of my life which only I knew, and some which I hadn't even known about myself until subsequent checking. Astonished, I asked how he knew those things about a complete stranger, and he replied, 'Your vibrations have no secrets.'

"After the first treatment I felt much better, and had a ravenous appetite. By the third day of treatments my head had returned to normal position. I continued taking energy treatments, but only a little at a time or I would pass out, and soon I was hired as bookkeeper for a large plywood company in the East Bay area, where I still work. During those years I would write my family about this wonderful man, and how much he had helped me and many others, but they could not comprehend it.

"Finally my mother came to San Francisco to 'see what hold this man has on my daughter,' but she was so astonished to observe my normal posture and radiant health that she went to Mr. A. Then he had the job of treating my eighty-one-year-old mother for glaucoma and a heart condition, and she was so excited about her prompt improvement that she wouldn't go back to Kansas either. She also wanted to be near him in order to receive the energies. At the age of three, my little niece was brought limp and almost lifeless to Mr. A, while in the grip of a severe asthma attack. She was struggling and fighting for breath, but after one treatment she was relieved, and now at age sixteen she enjoys a full and active life."

I asked Miss Hughes for her general impressions of Mr. A's work, and she replied, "At this Spring of 1972 I am sixty-three years old, and still working and enjoying a full life, which includes managing my six-room house and doing all the yard work. I am in excellent health and never miss a day's work at the office. Words cannot express my gratitude to Mr. A for all he has done for me."

These dramatic cases are by no means unique. During the seven years since Mr. A first walked into my house in Georgetown (Washington, D.C.) I have observed his work with numerous patients, have myself been treated by the healing life energies projected through his fingers, and have talked with hundreds of people who have been healed through his ministrations. More than ten thousand readers of *A Search for the Truth* have written to ask me about this remarkable healer and have pleaded to know more about his method of operation, his general philosophy, and the source of his healing knowledge.

After I became personally involved in the cases of Patricia Golden, little Larry Andrews, and several others, my own curiosity was whetted to know more about Mr. A and the life energies. Accordingly, I began to interview a large cross-section of his patients, and as I listened to their astonishing stories and examined their medical records, I realized that because of the magnitude of this man's contribution to humanity, his story should be told in depth.

# CHAPTER II

# In the Beginning

Who is this so-called miracle healer who can seemingly eradicate pain with the touch of his fingers? And how did he acquire his strange talent and awareness of the universal laws he calls the Ancient Wisdom?

Philip A (as I shall call him) was born to an Irish mother and Scotch-Irish father early in the morning of July 13, 1895, at their house in St. Paul, Minnesota. His mother Annie, then in her fifties, had given birth ten years earlier to a daughter, and fourteen years before that to a son. Phil was her change-of-life baby, and Mary Egan, an Irish friend who lived next door, subsequently told him, "You came into this life wrapped in several veils. Your mother took care of the whole situation herself, and then cooked breakfast for the family."

Annie was a character in her own right. The first born of Irish parents who had migrated to America from the Old Country during the potato famine, she was born in Covington, Kentucky, and reared by her father like a boy. He taught her to handle a gun effectively, and when at twenty-one she was old enough to file for homestead land, she set out alone into the wilderness of northern Minnesota, then newly admitted to the Union, to stake her claim near Wadena. In order to acquire permanent title to the land she had to occupy it for four years, after which she sent for her parents and their younger children. Turning the farm over to them, she then went on to Brainerd, Minnesota, to earn a living.

There she met her future husband, a native of New York State who had worked on railroad construction crews, in harvest fields and timber camps before opening a saloon in Brainerd, the legendary home of the giant Paul Bunyan. Ed A, Phil's future father, had the only safe in town, where lumberjacks would often store their valuables, and because he peaceably settled so many of their arguments, they respectfully addressed him as "Justice."

A few years after the birth of their first son, Ed and Annie moved to St. Paul, where their only daughter was born, and Annie was still a powerful woman six feet tall, weighing two hundred pounds, when Phil came along ten years later. The two-story house where he was born was a spacious place with five bedrooms and a sleeping porch, but like most Midwestern houses of its day it lacked central heating, and Phil vividly recalls the cold winter mornings when the children would all rush downstairs to dress beside the big old stove in the living room. Surrounded by oak trees, hazel brush, open fields, and a woods, it was a block from the nearest neighbor. In summer, when the gypsy caravans approached St. Paul, Phil's mother would run her chickens into the pen and the cow into the barn. Once, when some of the gypsy women became excited at seeing the star in Phil's right palm, which, in their tradition, suggests great psychic talent, Annie marched her youngest child into the house and told him to stay there whenever gypsies were in sight.

Phil, so much younger than his brother and sister, says that from his earliest recollection he was receiving a steady stream of instructions and explanations of life from the Powers, which he assumed was natural to everyone until he discovered that only puzzlement met him when he tried to discuss it with other children or adults. "Who told you that?" friends and relatives would demand, and Phil could only reply, "It just comes."

Because of the healing knowledge that has seemingly always been a part of him, it was natural he should try to ease the suffering of others. When a visiting uncle who had brought cattle to St. Paul complained of his "bad case of dysentery," Phil, still little more than a toddler, had a "flash" that told him blowfly eggs had gotten into some meat that his uncle had eaten along the road. Going to the cupboard, he stood on tiptoe to reach the epsom salts, mixed two tablespoons in a glass of water, and handed it to his uncle.

"Drink salts in my condition!" the uncle roared. "This kid must be crazy."

Phil's mother, by now aware of her son's strange powers, laughed. "I'd advise you to do what he says. Phil has a way that we don't understand."

Looking uneasy, the man downed the salts and the next morning reported that all traces of dysentery had vanished.

Another time, a neighbor woman who was visiting with Phil's mother complained of persistent stomach pains. The little boy, to whom ailing bodies have always meant machines that needed tuning and oiling, started to put his hand under her dress to send energy to her magnetic field, but was resoundingly slapped for his impertinence. Immediately afterward Annie summoned the family doctor, a bearded old gentleman in a frock coat who made his calls by horse and buggy, and told him what had happened. Then, pointing to her youngest child, she said, "Doctor, it belongs to me, but what am I going to do with it?"

"Look, lady," he replied, "if you don't know what to do with it, I do. I'm going to use it." Calling the youngster to his side, he asked, "How would you like to make my rounds with me and see the patients? I'll let you drive my team."

Ecstatic at the thought of driving the matched pair of horses, Phil joyfully assented, and afterward made frequent trips with the doctor, generating energy to some of his patients.

It must have been an unenviable task to be the mother of so unusual a child as Phil. He totally lacked fear, and he says that at the age of five he "began taking off for the lakes or the woods, staying away from home for several days at a time." His broad-shouldered mother could swing a hefty punch, and she often landed one on Phil's chin, but the boy remained unperturbed by punishment. He was listening to inner rather than outer instructions, and at the age of six he declared his emancipation: "Ma, I have my own life to live, and I mustn't have any interference with it." She must surely have wondered how she could have given birth to such an oddity, but from then on she grew accustomed to his sudden absences from home.

In those days, Buster Brown suits were high fashion

for little boys, and his mother bought one, complete with a large hat and shoes which buttoned up the sides. Over Phil's strenuous objections she dressed him in the new outfit, snapped some pictures of him, and then asked him to go to the store for her. Phil pleaded for permission to remove the "sissy suit" first, but strong-willed Annie ordered him to go just as he was. As Phil recalls, "On the way to the grocery, I ran into a group of local kids, and that was the end of my Buster Brown. When I returned home, it was in shreds."

Yet Phil must have been an engaging child, for neighbors and strangers had a habit of indulging him. There were numerous lakes within three to eight miles of his home, and at one of them a man would let him row a boat all day in exchange for bailing out his other boats. Like most boys Phil was perpetually hungry, but food came easily to him. On the lakes he would catch muskies, pickerel, and sunfish; then bake them in the sand under a fire or fry them on a piece of tin he had polished with a rock. Sometimes farmers would invite him in for a glass of milk and piece of cake, and he was known throughout the area as "Ed's boy," although his father frequently did not know his whereabouts.

"It was nice to be off by myself," Mr. A reminisces. "I felt better when I was, and there were deer and other animals in the woods who seemed very tame. I loved that life. All the while I was alone, Life and the History of Life were being explained to me in detail, through inner listening. That was my education. What I was receiving was not taught in any schools."

For instance, at the dinner table one day Phil's older

41

brother and sister were discussing the mysterious construction of the Great Pyramid in Egypt, and they quoted a newspaper article as saying that Napoleon's entire army could not have moved one of those tremendous stones from its original site to its place in the pyramid. Phil, absorbed in his food, remarked casually, "It was really quite simple. The people at that time knew nature's secret of hardening sand in the same way that the earth does it. They simply made forms and filled them with sand, and mixed the hardening solution in it. Then, after it solidified, they polished the top of each block to prevent deterioration or seepage, and then formed another block on top of it in the same manner." His family sat stunned, looking from one to another, but said no more. They were becoming accustomed to these strange explanations from little Phil.

Meanwhile his father was running a wholesale business, and his mother was guarding the home front, sometimes with the .38 revolver she slipped into a pocket under her apron. Their haystacks were near the Great Northern Railroad tracks, and occasionally tramps, or "road gentlemen," would sleep there until Annie appeared brandishing her gun. "I'm not going to have you smoking around my haystacks," she would explain. Once she drove off three men so dramatically that they dropped some papers as they fled. On examining them, Annie called the police, who immediately sent out an inspector.

"You were real lucky, ma'am," the official told Annie. "Those were the men we've been looking for who robbed a bank yesterday and killed the teller."

Phil remembers his mother's calm reply, "No, mister, *they* were lucky. If they'd made one false move, I would have shot an ear off."

Some years later, while visiting his mother's youngest brother in Billings, Montana, Phil was asked, "Does your mother ever do any shooting?"

"The only time I ever saw her pull a trigger," Phil replied, "was when my brother was using her .38 revolver to try to hit a cowbell on a fence post. Ma was feeding the chickens, but she watched him miss three times. Then she took the gun from him, and while still straightening up from a stooping position she fired. The cowbell left the post, and as she handed the gun back, she sighed, 'To think I have a son who can't shoot a gun!' and walked into the house."

Phil's uncle grinned broadly and exclaimed, "So she still has that .38 of hers! She was a real marksman in her day—could shoot the head off a bird in flight with a rifle. She's won a lot of trophies. Did you ever know your mother was a deputy sheriff and famous with a gun?"

On Phil's next visit home he challenged his mother with the story, and she was furious that he knew about it; but she finally consented to show him her trophies, buried deep in the lower compartment of an old trunk in the attic.

Phil started school the fall after his sixth birthday, but the routine bored him. Mathematics and history came easily, but he simply could not comprehend reading, writing, and spelling. It was as if a curtain cloaked his mind in those classes, and even today he can scarcely read and spell, although if he skims a book's first couple of pages, he seems able intuitively to tell you what the remainder is about.

As a child he always had pets, but his teachers were not amused when the gophers he frequently carried in his pockets escaped into the classroom. He was more adept at playing hooky than studying, and in the wintertime he says that he "lived on ice skates" at Como Lake near his house.

One day he found two wolf cubs in the woods and brought them home, but was not allowed to keep them. He gave them to a friend, and, as he watched them grow, it occurred to him that where a collie has long hind legs for speed, the wolf has a stronger chest which should be good for pulling. At the proper time, Phil bred a friend's collie to one of the wolves, and selected a pup from the litter to train as a lead dog. From the age of seven to twelve, Phil had a paper route for the St. Paul *Daily News*, and did the collecting for a much larger area, using a bicycle in summer and his dog and sled in winter. Shep, half collie and half wolf, was trained to help with the route, and while Phil delivered papers to the doors, Shep would pull the sled to the next distribution point and wait for him, becoming so adept at it that the newspaper carried a picture of Phil and his accomplished lead dog.

After Phil had had the route for a couple of years, an adult solicitor spent three days combing his territory for new customers, and added fourteen. Then the newspaper sponsored a contest for carriers, offering prizes for a specified number of new customers, and the youngster combed the same route a second time, adding eighty new clients. The circulation manager, aware that one of his best salesmen had recently called on all the residents, challenged Phil's

44

figures. But when all checked out, he asked the boy how he had managed it.

"To tell you the truth," the boy confessed, "I had to play hooky three days to do it, so I've been kicked out of school." The circulation manager took Phil to see the superintendent of schools, explained the situation, and managed to have him reinstated. For his grandiose success Phil carried off all the newspaper prizes, including a 17-jewel Elgin watch in an 18-carat gold case, a gray sweater, a pair of ice skates, a big flashlight, and two season tickets to the Orpheum Theater. For once in his life, he was the school hero.

# CHAPTER III

# The Universal Ring

Mr. A had an active and in many ways typical boyhood for those turn-of-the-century years when our land and waters were unpolluted, when "book learning" seemed less important than fishing or helping out in the grain fields, and when many youngsters left school at thirteen or fourteen to earn a living. Yet there was always something different about Phil which set him apart from his playmates, and he tries to express it this way: "For as long as I can remember I was receiving a continual flow of information coming over the air from The Universal Ring of Wisdom, explaining the Ancient Wisdoms of life, and I was receiving instructions pertaining to the generation of human energy. Receiving this information was always as constant and natural to me as breathing, but it was a puzzlement to my family, and particularly to my older brother who would question me almost endlessly, wanting to know how I had derived certain knowledge. Often these sessions would continue throughout the night. I would answer my brother's questions to the best of my ability and promptly fall asleep. He would study my answers, and then awaken me with more questions."

In preparing this book, I too asked how he derived

his information, and Mr. A replied, "Why, from tuning in on The Ring." Pressed to explain in terms available to the layman, he said that a protective ring of energy encircles each planet and stores within it all knowledge since time began. All thoughts and inventions, he said, are "taken off The Ring," and all such information is available to anyone who learns to listen. He says that the Ancient Wisdom implanted in his mind as a child is unchanging. The years have merely expanded it and brought to him increasing proof of all he learned as a boy.

"The theory of energy as the life-force and body activity is as old as the ages," he continues, "and there are many well versed in the Ancient Wisdom to whom most of this is known. This world we live in is composed of gases and energy. All substance—plant, animal, and human life—results from the unlimited combination of energy frequencies acting on these gases. Every plant, animal, and human has its own individual energy frequency to establish and maintain life, growth, and development. At birth, the first breath of life is our direct supply, our lifeline with the Universal Power . . . Life itself! At any time that this energy flow is cut off from the magnetic field, the energy which originally sets the field becomes a part of the Power it came from. So long as this energy is established and flows through without obstruction, we are in tune with the Universal supply of energy."

Mr. A says that in the lower abdomen is the master brain, an intricate system forming the magnetic field, "the grouping together of the main trunk nerves with their branches and relay systems extending throughout the entire body." Normally, he explains, the magnetic field gives the lungs the strength to pull in all of the energies. But the field in turn draws its personal energy frequency from the lungs to itself, for distribution throughout the body. He says that some of the symptoms of insufficient energy distribution are shortness of breath, nervousness, confusion, restlessness, irritability, bloat, pain, and a feeling of heaviness. Their intensity depends on the degree of depletion of the magnetic field, which is caused by fear, anger, hatred, shock, or improper or deficient nerve fueling.

"A child is born with a strong or a weak nervous system," he says, "which is determined at conception and is the result of his parents' energies. If the mother and father are of mated frequencies and are well and strong at the time the child is conceived, that child ordinarily has an easy birth and a strong, healthy nervous system. If the child is the result of mismated energy currents, and the future parents are nervous, discontented, or unhealthy, the baby usually has a weak nervous system, and may also have a difficult delivery. Because of this, he is the victim of low energy and nerve depletion for most of his life. But even when a child inherits a weak magnetic field, that tension can be released shortly after birth by someone with the properly blended energy who is able to convey this energy to the infant's magnetic field so that the infant is freed from bondage and open to the universe, and is thereby able to draw his normal capacity of energy from the atmosphere."

Who is that person? Mr. A says that the individual with a strong, healthy nervous system generates enough fuel or energy to maintain his own requirements and automatically to radiate a strong surplus.

Such a person is best equipped to help others and can be taught, according to Mr. A, how to direct the energy, feed nerves, and release nerve spasms in a person with an energy pattern blending with his own. But apparently there are not many people like Mr. A, who on placing his ear to a patient's chest automatically recognizes his energy pattern and adjusts his own pattern to the ailing one's.

To illustrate, several patients will claim that a certain masseuse is able to massage, relax, and relieve their pain to such an extent that they may experience relief lasting for several weeks or even permanently, while others may get little or no relief from exactly the same masseuse. Mr. A says that those receiving benefit have blending energies, and while being massaged and without realizing it, are fed their required current and nerve energy from the masseuse, who is so strong in energy that she can feed it to others. But if a patient has a differing nerve energy, not only she but also the masseuse may feel sapped and exhausted after a treatment. Throughout our lifetime, according to Mr. A, the nervous system is constantly influenced by the energy from all human contacts. Some radiate energy for us, while others drain it from us.

Mr. A asserts that physical characteristics occur at conception, and one's individuality is determined at birth, with the first breath taken representing the influence exerted by the three ruling solar suns, known originally as the Trinity, which are a part of the Power of Powers. This combination of the energy from each sun, at different frequencies, establishes one's very life: the magnetic field.

I asked Phil who God is, and he replied, "The

Power of Powers." Pressed to elaborate on the magnetic field, he continued, "There are compatible, neutral, and negative types of energy. Compatible, or matching, energies together generate revitalizing energy for magnetic fuel. Compatible human energies as a rule are of the same group: earth with earth, fire with fire, air with air, and water with water, providing the individuals are of a different birth month but matching frequency, although many variations occur because of the different planetary positions for each individual at birth.

"Negative human energies are those of different elements, such as combining earth with air, fire with water, etc. In general, their combined action causes a depletion of the magnetic field at different levels, thereby losing its drawing power on human energy taken in by the lungs. Neutral human energies are earth with earth, fire with fire, etc., when the individuals are of the same birth month and do not have other complementary energies. They ordinarily do not refuel one another. They blend and act as one element, or duplicate type. With a depletion in the magnetic field, the proper amount of fuel is not taken in, and slow starvation of the nervous system continues while they are together. These are, of course, only the general principles and there are finer gradations when applied to the individual, taking into consideration the rising sign and the exact position of the planets at the moment of birth. There are many other facets of fueling energy patterns."

Having only the vaguest notion of what Mr. A was talking about, I consulted an astrology book and read that those born in Aries are under the fire sign; Taurus, earth, Gemini, air; Cancer, water; Leo, fire; Virgo, earth; Libra, air; Scorpio, water; Sagittarius, fire; Capricorn, earth; Aquarius, air; Pisces, water.

Mr. A says that our nervous system, through our magnetic field, is influenced by every person with whom we come in contact. "This constantly has its effect on one's magnetic field, thereby affecting the nervous system," he explains. "If one's own generation of energy is strong, these cross energies from others have little or no effect on our nerves. If we are weakened or depleted, reaction is likely. This interaction of energy fields is greatly emphasized in the handling of a new baby. In the growing child, his needed feeding of the nerves must come by radiation from his close associates, and is strengthened or depleted by them. If the child's energy current blends with that of his father or mother he will instinctively seek to be with that parent as much as possible, because he is soothed and nourished by him; but when the energies are in opposition, there is nervousness and friction between parent and child. If both parents oppose his energy pattern, a problem child may develop who is delicate and high-strung, and whose nature is a mystery to his parents.

"Sometimes a child is thin, nervous, and irritable because of this condition, but after he starts school he may become reasonable and energetic because he has instinctively selected playmates who have blending energy and can act as fuel for his magnetic field. If he fails to find such companions, he will prefer to play alone. If such a child eventually marries a person of correctly mated energy, his depleted nerves will rapidly be restored, and within a few years his personality and conduct will have been transformed. With a relaxed nervous system, his prospects of health and success are greatly enhanced, but if he marries one of an opposing energy, his magnetic field is partially depleted. Starvation of the nerves occurs, and within a short time he finds himself beset by restlessness and discontent. When the natural mating current is absent, people are aware of an insatiable craving, a craving they often seek to satisfy with too much food or drink, believing it will give them energy or strength. But the beneficial results are nil. Their nerves are not being fed, by not complying with the laws of nature."

The strange talent with which Mr. A was born is the power to rebuild the nervous system, relieve the pressures and tensions, and correct ailments by energizing the magnetic field. He accomplishes this by placing his fingers over nerves and nerve relay centers, automatically generating the energy complementary to that of the patient. As a generator he has the knack of increasing the intensity of the energy to make corrections, and this life energy that he transmits is said to be several times greater than the mating-energy between people. This generated energy is not the same as mechanically generated electrical current. He says that the body is not geared to accept the latter, which the nerves will not retain and which acts as a shock to them. To rebuild nerves, to relax spasms and feed the required energy fuel, the energies of the generator must match or synchronize with those of the patient. It is Mr. A's rare ability to be able to match those energies.

When one undergoes treatment by Mr. A, one's

first sensation is of a mild vibration at the point where his hand touches. Then the vibrations begin shooting up or down to the area of the body that cries for attention. The patient may groan and grab a sore shoulder, but Mr. A has not touched it. The energy is magically flowing through it from the contact point, and after a few minutes one is soothed by a mild heat penetrating every part of the body. Instead of breathing shallowly from the chest, one will discover that he is breathing deeply, as if from the pelvic region. Pain vanishes, and when Mr. A tells him to raise an arm or leg that has been immobile for months or years, it will shoot up effortlessly, without a twinge of pain.

Those of us who have experienced Mr. A's seemingly miraculous curative powers tend to press him, "Why doesn't everyone know about this revolutionary new method of treating physical disorders?"

"Revolutionary? New?" he asks, with a warm smile. "No, this theory is as old as the world. It is simply a lost art. The Bible records that some people in ancient days, and some in the New Testament had the understanding and wisdom of healing through the laying on of hands. It's my opinion that this was their method of distributing human energy. The Power that passes through my hands resides in everyone. Only the knowledge of its application is necessary. I of myself do nothing. The Power does the work. I am merely a distributor."

From birth to adolescence, Mr. A declares, the body receives nerve fuel by radiation from others, but during adolescence the body's requirements change. For continued smooth functioning, the nervous system demands a greater supply of its own energy, plus a mating energy.

"This nerve fueling takes place normally during the sex relationship with a person having properly mated energies," he continues. "This is nature's method of keeping the magnetic field vital. Nature's purpose is reproduction of the race, and nerve fueling is imperative through normal sex life without insulation, in order to maintain health. Unfortunately, many people after a certain point in life discontinue this natural relationship, not realizing they are inviting nerve depletion and starvation, and thus ailments and abnormal function. One of the main fueling nerves in relation to the magnetic field of women is the clitoris nerve. When this nerve is dormant it does not properly relay fuel to the magnetic field. With a partial dormancy of the field, there is insufficient distribution of the energy, and nervous tension increases. Over a period of time symptoms appear, revealing the malfunctioning of the body. Too often, these unfortunate people are called neurotics.

"This dormancy in a woman also has its effects on the nervous system of the male. As he receives an insufficient amount of his required nerve fuel from the woman, his own nervous system begins to react from starvation of nerve energy. Tension, irritability, and friction may result. Women are more likely than men to be subject to a partial dormancy of the magnetic field. This dormancy can be caused by shock or injury to the clitoris often sustained during the first sex act. This is usually owing to the lack of understanding of how important these nerves are to life, health, and contentment.

"As a rule a woman is slower to animate than a man, but when stimulated she will automatically start generating. However, she must receive the generation in return from her partner. He should have the wisdom to generate energy to her in order to complete the revitalization of their magnetic fields. Otherwise she, being the more sensitive, will eventually cease generating to him and accept the act solely as a marital duty.

"Fueling of the magnetic field may also cease as a result of opposing energies. When the wave energies are not properly blended, there follows a sense of dissatisfaction or depletion which many people do not understand. Every parent has had to meet the problems of explaining sex to the growing, inquisitive child. But how many parents understand the purpose behind it all? Prevention of ailments through understanding is always the best remedy, and that prevention lies in teaching our children."

In order to help me understand what Mr. A was attempting to describe concerning the nerve depletion existing in some marriages, a nurse who has worked closely with him for a number of years offered to give me an example of a mismated couple: "I followed this case with interest," she began, "because it was the first of its kind to come to my personal attention. When the husband first came to Mr. A he had all the symptoms of critical illness, but after a course of treatments he became healthy and normal in every way. He was a fire wave energy and his wife was an earth wave energy. As a consequence, each had depleted the other. Here, let me show you the records on the case."

Pulling a signed statement from her files, she

handed me a copy of the man's unsolicited testimonial, which reads in part: "I was sick before I began taking these treatments. I had a bad back and heart, and everything was the matter with me. I had been seeing a doctor for some time but was steadily getting worse. I was taking shots twice a week, and finally every day, but I continually grew weaker. I had reached the point where I could not eat or sleep. After the first treatment here I could breathe more deeply, and after I left Mr. A's office I felt hungry for the first time in years, so I went to a restaurant and ordered a steak. It was good and I was still hungry, so I had a second one. I haven't missed a meal since, and after the third visit I began to feel wonderful. After ten treatments I was completely well, and although my work isn't easy I haven't missed a day on the job since."

The man brought his wife to Mr. A, who as soon as he had listened to her chest automatically understood the cause of her difficulty. She was frail and nervous and spent much of her time in bed despite constant treatments from her family doctor. When the nurse put her fingers on the woman's pulse, she said that the heart was "wild," rapid and irregular, and her breathing fast and shallow.

She remembers that Mr. A said, "We'll revitalize your field before we tune the motor." After a short time he instructed the nurse to put her fingers on the woman's pulse. "The quality of her pulse changed first," the nurse told me. "It became stronger when he generated the energy to the area of her chest, and soon the pulse began to slow down. The volume and quality improved, and the beat grew more regular. In about three minutes her pulse was beating at a normal rhythm and rate, her respiration slowed and became deeper, and her face lost its look of strain. At the end of several visits she was transformed—relaxed, smiling, and rested. She and her husband were glowing with happiness when they said good-bye, and they still drop in occasionally for a recharge, since they now understand about the mismated energy patterns."

Another case in the files recalls a woman suffering from what Mr. A describes as "lack of required mating fuel." After five treatments, the patient wrote this report: "I don't remember how many doctors I had actually consulted, but each gave me a different opinion. I thought I had stomach trouble because I had had severe pains in my stomach for years, and when I had an attack my abdomen would swell out until I could hardly breathe. Every doctor I saw wanted to operate, but each for a different reason. None seemed to know what was wrong with me. For the past year I have had severe pains in the back of my legs. Four months ago I had an attack in my back which was sheer torture. A doctor treated me, but the pain became so much worse that I discontinued the treatments.

"Then a neighbor told me about this kind of human energy treatment, and simply to please her I came to Mr. A. I was badly swollen, hardly able to breathe, and too sick to care what happened to me. Mr. A didn't have his fingers on me for more than ten seconds when he said, 'Now, where is your stomach?' I looked down and the swelling was totally gone. It was miraculous! I was flat again and could breathe deeply for the first time in three years. The pains in my legs disappeared after the first treatment and have never recurred. I feel simply wonderful!"

I sought an explanation from Mr. A, and he said, "Just another manifestation of nerves in spasm from lack of proper mating fuel. The depleted magnetic field affected the nerve supply to the stomach and intestines. The resulting spasm of the nerves created a ballooning of the bowel, producing the tension that caused the pain and distress that brought her here. When the correct energy was generated to her magnetic field, the abdominal swelling disappeared in a matter of seconds. With the spasm and tension released she could breathe deeply, bring a full supply of her own energy wave into her magnetic field, and send this energy to her entire nervous system, which relieved all pain. Simple, isn't it?"

Simple, yes . . . if you are born with Mr. A's gift of healing.

# CHAPTER IV

## The Lean Years

I first met Mr. A in February, 1966, when the beautiful American wife of a European ambassador brought him to my house in Washington. Before me stood a massively built, youngish-looking man with clear, unlined skin. Today his skin remains as unmarked by age as a twenty-year-old, except for his laugh wrinkles, and his palms resemble those of any youngster who has never done a day's hard work, were it not for the clearly defined star in the right palm. Yet he is now seventy-seven, and his life has been crammed with manual labor, joyously performed.

On that chill winter day, the ambassador's wife told me Mr. A had corrected a "leaking heart valve" which had bothered her since birth. She said that three doctors were present at her first meeting with Mr. A, listening to her heartbeat and confirming its irregularity. Then Mr. A placed his fingers on a spot behind her upper shoulder, "and when the doctors listened to my heart action again, they were nearly overcome with shock. They said it sounded as smooth as the motor of a Rolls-Royce. Now I can go anywhere without having to guard against a strain on my heart. It has changed my whole life."

I asked Mr. A how he had effected such a seeming

miracle, and he replied, "We reground the valves. We simply opened the switches, strengthened her magnetic field, tuned her motor, let the energy current through, burned out the rust, and oiled a few joints in the course of several treatments."

When I laughingly remarked that he sounded like a master mechanic, his blue eyes danced as he replied, "I used to be one." I later learned that this was indeed true, and that he can repair a delicate piece of machinery as easily as a leaking heart valve. That era of his life began at the family supper table when Phil, who was fourteen and had quit school after the fourth grade, heard his father say, "A fine bunch of kids I've got. You'd starve to death if I didn't feed you."

"You mean me?" Phil asked, aware that his older brother and sister were both working and taking university courses at night.

Glumly, his father replied, "I mean *all* of you." Nothing further was said, but the next morning Phil answered an advertisement for "machinist and apprentice wanted," and was told, "It's going to be rough and tough, lad, but you've got the job if you can take it. The pay will be ten cents an hour, ten hours a day and five hours on Saturday."

That first day Phil worked in the blacksmith shop, handling the sledge for ten hours while the head machinist was forge-welding steel for elevator frames. The next day the new apprentice was running a bolt-threading machine, and the following day he turned a shafting to different sizes on a lathe. Not yet full grown, he lacked the height to reach the calipers, so the foreman provided a slab of timber for him to stand on.

Phil rented a room over a piano factory and for several months subsisted principally on canned beans and bread, until he returned home as a paying boarder. After only six months' experience as an apprentice, he was put in full charge of installing the elevators in buildings, still at ten cents a hour. Later he was hired away by International Harvester Company at more than twice his salary, as an apprentice machinist.

But Phil wanted to see more of the world than St. Paul. At twenty-one he became night foreman of the machine shop at Armour's, next a machinist repairing stokers on the Great Northern Railroad, and later a machinist for the rotogravure presses at Brown & Bigelow's printing company. All the while he was inventing more efficient tools to do his assigned jobs, but a lathe-cutting tool which he fashioned to sweep across the five-foot doctor blade of the rotogravure presses proved his undoing. When the management discovered how radically this simplified the work, they gave his job to a boy at fifteen dollars a week.

Phil next became a salesman, peddling everything from barber supplies and pine Christmas wreaths to carpeting and paint spray guns. Phenomenally successful, he invariably became sales manager for whatever product he was handling at the time, and his travels eventually took him to every state in the Union. Whenever in the vicinity of St. Paul he would stop off to see his mother, by then widowed, and once when she was entertaining relatives for dinner, a cousin asked if it bothered her to have Phil roaming all over the country and never to know where he was.

"He can take care of himself," she replied, "but I've always told him that a rolling stone gathers no moss."

From across the table, Phil countered, "Yes, but did you ever see how that stone gets polished?" Annie, who was cutting bread at the time, threw the loaf at him.

Always Phil listened to his "inner instructions," which told him that he must learn more about people and life, and on his travels he was learning rapidly. In the spring of 1926 he bought a Willys automobile and converted it into a camping rig. "By lifting the front seat an inch," he recalls, "it would flatten into a bed. I built in a pantry with icebox and made frames with mosquito netting for the windows so that I could sleep and eat in the car." At this time he was selling spray guns to used-car dealers, and he found that he could cover four to six towns a day, calling on dealers, and still have time for the fishing expeditions he loved.

"That summer I got married," he reminisces, "and we started on our honeymoon, camping and selling as we went, but my wife didn't care for camping. Also, she insisted on telling me all about how she and my mother had gotten into one of my suitcases in the attic and read letters from many of the girls I'd met in my travels. She wouldn't stop raising hell about them, so after the third day of this, I pulled into the railroad station of a town we were passing through. She asked, 'What are you doing here?' and I replied, 'You're going back to St. Paul, and I'm going on my own honeymoon.' Putting her on the train, I headed off to my selling trip before returning to St. Paul.

"Not long afterwards my territory was enlarged

to include the Dakotas, Montana, Idaho, Washington, and Oregon. In November my wife and I started out for the West Coast, planning to spend the winter in Washington and Oregon while I covered that territory. We had to fight bad weather all the way: snow, mud, rain, and slippery roads. It was hard on a girl who wasn't used to that kind of arduous traveling, and she was petrified. She hated to ride in a car after dark, but after leaving Billings, Montana, the snow was coming down so heavily I had to ignore her fuming and demands that we stop for the night. My inner instructions told me we should go on to Bozeman. We arrived there after midnight, and the next day's newspaper reported that the road we had just come over was now closed for the winter.

"The next day, more snow and mud, but we finally made it to Spokane, Washington, where the Davenport Hotel seemed so much like heaven that we stayed for a week, resting up. Leaving Spokane, we drove to Seattle and rented an apartment, because my wife was pregnant. Then, after I had covered my northern territory, we went down to Los Angeles, taking another apartment, and I continued to sell."

Their daughter was born August 14, 1927, and later that fall Phil received a letter, forwarded to him by his mother, which contained a railroad ticket from St. Paul to California and a check for two hundred dollars. The letter read, "Come out and see what is wrong with my business." It was signed "C. Hill, MD" and Phil's "inner instructions" told him to heed the blunt summons.

Phil continued as a salesman in the Los Angeles area until his daughter was old enough to travel. Then they started north, with the baby lying in a hammock suspended above the back seat of the car. At that time it took two days to drive to the Bay Area over the old Ridge Route, and on arriving Phil rented a duplex. When he made inquiries about C. Hill, MD, he learned the doctor was a well-liked professional of impeccable reputation, who owned a hospital.

Phil liked Dr. Hill on sight, but the tall, gray-haired, handsome physician looked puzzled when Phil returned the money and railroad ticket, explaining that he had driven from Los Angeles instead of taking a train from St. Paul.

Dr. Hill said he had approximately three thousand acres of swampland near Mendin, Nevada, which he hoped to turn into a muskrat farm. "I've been wanting to go into the fur business in a big way, with tanning and manufacturing," he told Phil, "and from what I've heard about you, you're the man who can put this over."

They were chatting in the office of Dr. Hill's hospital when the physician was summoned to the operating room. Unexpectedly, he said to Phil, "I want you to come and watch me operate. This case is a referral, a woman with a large cyst, a 'pregnancy' that has gone to eleven months."

Watching him operate, Phil wondered why the doctor had wanted him along. Then he saw him "start tightening his arm and manipulating his elbow on her chest in the heart area."

"Are you trying to give her energy?" Phil asked, impulsively.

Glancing up, the doctor replied, "What do you

know about energy? If you know a damn thing about it, get busy!"

Mr. A quickly put his hand beneath the sheet, on the woman's left side, and sent a charge of energy surging through her. Immediately her shallow breathing became normal. Back in the office, the doctor looked silently at Phil for a time before booming, "That's the best damn display of energy I've ever seen. You're good! I heard about you from my mother-in-law in Minnesota. I'd like to open your work to the world, but they would hang you." He paused thoughtfully and then continued, "But from here on you are my business adviser. This way you'll be available when I need you. After what I saw today, I'm sure that the energy can eliminate weakness and pain after surgery. As soon as my patients awaken we can get them into motion and on their feet, so I won't have to worry about blood clots. And I'm convinced today's episode could have been avoided if that woman had had that energy you gave her *before* the operation."

Thereafter, Phil frequently revitalized the magnetic fields of Dr. Hill's patients, but one day the physician's son drove him out to see the future muskrat farm, and also to the gambling casinos of Reno, where Phil promptly lost eighty-three dollars at the crap table.

"I've got to work this out," he thought, and as soon as he returned to his hotel room he begin rolling a pair of dice until he was convinced he had evolved a winning system. Then he returned to the casino, promptly recovered his lost money and thirty dollars more. During the Depression that was soon to come,

67

Phil's "system" was more than once to rescue him and his business associates from foreclosure or near-starvation.

Shortly before the stock market crash of 1929, when the fur farm was booming, Phil had one of his peculiar inward flashes which told him to cash in his stocks. He promptly did so and advised Dr. Hill, who was heavily invested on margin at a bank, to do likewise. Pulling a long face, the handsome old doctor said, "I've gone along with you on all of your other suggestions, but not this one."

"I'm out of it, and I'm advising you to get out now," Phil repeated, but the next day the stock went up and Dr. Hill laughed at him. "Now, you see, if I had followed your advice what would I have lost?"

Phil said, "I'm still telling you to get out right away, and I hope you will." The next day the bottom dropped out of the market. Money became as scarce as the proverbial hen's teeth, but Dr. Hill gamely continued his long-standing policy of performing a necessary operation first and talking about possible payment afterward. Consquently, no money was coming in to his hospital, but Dr. Hill and Phil had previously subdivided forty acres which the doctor owned on the California side of Lake Tahoe and he had offered to split 60/40 with Phil on any lots that he could sell. To do so Phil needed a real estate broker's license, and his secretary warned him that the examination was so tough that even brilliant lawyers had failed.

"You can't spell, let alone read," she pointed out, "so you might as well save your time." Phil, knowing he had no choice except to sell the lots, took the examination while relying almost entirely on his inner instructions for the answers. To his secretary's amazement, he passed. He then began selling lake lots, at a time when nothing else was moving on the real estate market, and depositing the doctor's share in a bank account Phil opened for him.

Late in 1930 Dr. Hill, now in his late sixties, told him that the creditors were demanding a meeting, because the hospital had no money to pay them, despite the fact that a hundred thousand dollars in assets were on the books, if only the patients could settle their accounts.

"Why don't you pay off the creditors?" Phil asked laconically.

"With what?" Dr. Hill snapped.

"With the money you have in the bank."

"What money in the bank?"

"Well now," Phil said, "I've been depositing your sixty percent from the sales at the lake."

"You mean you've sold some lots? How many?" Dr. Hill asked excitedly.

"Nearly half the subdivision," Phil replied.

"Whew!" the doctor shouted and rushed out the door, doing a waltz turn with every nurse in sight up and down the corridor.

In the spring, with the Depression in full sway, Phil drove to Phoenix in the hope of finding an opportunity to work out some details concerning the muskrat business. While sitting in a restaurant he saw a woman at a nearby table who seemed so sad that he remarked, "You look as if the world has folded up on you."

"You would, too," she replied, "if you'd received the news I've just had from my doctors. I have one collapsed lung, and now they tell me that the other is spotted. It means the desert for me, and being a nurse, I know the significance of that. I don't have long to live."

"As bad as that?" Mr. A asked sympathetically, and after further discussion he offered to do what he could to help her. With the first treatment, she was bewildered by the new sense of bodily freedom which followed what Phil called "the recharge of your batteries." During the next two days he gave her five more charges of energy to revitalize her magnetic field and strengthen the lung tissue. That evening he was standing at the hotel desk when he was suddenly grabbed from behind and swung around so excitedly that he lost his balance and fell, with the woman on top of him.

"Will you kindly get off me?" he muttered in embarrassment, while she babbled that he must go with her to see her doctor. "I've just come from there," she explained, "and the new X rays show that my lungs are no longer spotted or collapsed. The doctors are mystified and want to know how you did it."

Instead, Phil headed for El Paso, where he began conducting long-distance experiments with Dr. Hill on sending energy through the air to the physician's patients in the Bay Area. These were experiments Phil had worked out at the age of eleven under "inner instruction," and Dr. Hill was sending back enthusiastic reports on the improvement of patients who received the "charge" at specified times.

Before he'd left for Phoenix, Phil and his wife had separated. Phil, firmly convinced that each person should be permitted to "operate his own planet," was plagued by her constant jealousy, and he says of that trying period, "Even when my daughter showed me affection, her mother would flare up at her, saying, 'You're just a chip off the old block.' "

Phil adored his little daughter, who like himself had a clearly defined star in her right palm, and whom he had taught to direct the energies; but his wife resented their closeness and forbade the child to use her healing abilities.

"Realizing the marriage wouldn't work," Phil says, "I moved into one of the hospital rooms, letting her have the duplex with our daughter. She filed suit, claiming I was not supporting her, but after the district attorney told me what I should be paying her each month, I showed him the cancelled checks proving I had been sending her considerably *more* than that amount. I then gave my wife checks dated for several months in advance, before making the trip to Phoenix."

During Phil's absence Dr. Hill operated on the varicose veins that had long been bothering him, not trusting anyone else to perform the operation. Shortly afterward, hospitalized with blood poisoning and pneumonia, he went into a coma and died before Phil could learn of his illness. Dr. Hill, who never seemed to think of his own ailments, had simply neglected to tell Phil of the condition.

"Never had anything hit me harder," Phil declares. "This man was under my skin and I thought a great deal of him. During the four years together we had worked out and proven many forms and formations of the energy pertaining to surgery, and although he didn't want to reveal his part in it at the time, he used to say, 'Someday I hope the world will understand and accept your work, for the good of humanity.' "

Phil had loved Dr. Hill like a second father, and after his death Phil helped to prevent foreclosure of the hospital, in behalf of Dr. Hill's family.

For many years Phil admired an attractive piece of land at Lake Tahoe, which was in two counties and comprised more than six hundred acres. On inquiry he learned that the original owner of the property, now deceased, had willed it to his three sons with an undivided interest but that subsequently one son drank himself to death, another committed suicide, and the surviving son, John, found his interests tied up with the two other unsettled estates. Mr. A says of the situation: "In the fall of 1931 John had come to me, asking if I would help unravel this highly complicated estate, which everyone else was calling The Impossible. I asked why he'd come to me, and he said, 'Well, it just seems like I have to, and you are the only one I can trust to protect my interests.' I said I would like to help but that I didn't have the time right then. However, after terminating my dealings at the hospital in the early part of 1932, I received inner instructions to take on the challenge of straightening out John's estate. This was to be my legal education and seasoning, in preparation for my main life's work which was to begin some nine years later.

"In the depth of the Depression, with no money and practically no educational background, I knew I would have to depend entirely on my inner instructions in order to cope with the legal and financial power that would oppose John's interests. I was informed by these inner sources that it would be an involved, perplexing, yet fascinating test of intuition, which some call ESP but, to me, means instruction from the Universal Ring of Wisdom. I therefore contacted John, who informed me that foreclosure proceedings had already been brought against his portion of the estate. In those Depression years, the only place where there seemed to be any money was at the gambling tables of Reno, and I was fortunate enough to win sufficient money to be able to delay foreclosure on John's interests. Many attorneys had previously tried their hand at disentangling the cords which bound John's property to his deceased brothers' but had eventually pronounced the situation insoluble. Everyone despaired except Mr. A, who had no legal background and could barely read and spell.

Another book could be written about Mr. A's life as a supersalesman and as a successful land developer at Lake Tahoe, where by following his "inner instructions" he overcame nearly insurmountable odds to win John's inheritance for him. That is the book Phil would like best, because healing comes so naturally to him that he does not even find it interesting to talk about. But he does take pride in his business successes, and he looks unhappy when I tell him, "Phil, nobody cares whether you ever sold a lot at Lake Takoe or unraveled a legal mare's nest. People want to know about your miraculous cures."

"There's no such thing as a miracle," he says with a sigh. "All anyone has to do is obey the natural laws of the Power of Powers. The Powers make no concession for the lack of knowledge of these laws."

For the several Depression years, following his "inner instructions," that he worked at the problem of John's estate money was virtually nonexistent, and he had to eat. The stories he tells probably sound funnier now than when he had to live through them, but he recalls: "I rented an old farmhouse near Auburn, surrounded by a pear orchard and other fruit trees, plus rows of currant, raspberry, and boysenberry bushes. With all this fruit and berries ripening, I decided to can them, and when the word spread, amused farm women came from the surrounding area to offer their pet recipes. I would go to the wholesale house in Sacramento and buy cases of Mason jars and hundred-pound sacks of sugar. I was told the pears had to be picked green four or five days before they were ripe, and spread out under cover, so I blanketed the floor of two of the rooms with pears. Then I had to go to Oakland on business, and when I returned they were all ripe. This meant I had to work twenty-four hours without sleep to get them canned. I even had to put them in ice water to keep them from going to mush before I could get all of them in the jars."

Phil was feeding a lot of workmen besides himself, and on Saturdays before the produce house in Sacramento closed for the weekend, prices on perishable items were marked down, so he could fill his car for a few dollars. After he started canning, just buying the sugar and jars kept him broke. But his mechanical ingenuity never deserted him. When he decided to make bread-and-butter pickles, after slicing "half a lug" of cucumbers and looking at the mountainous pile still confronting him, he fashioned an ingenious gadget with blades. Set over a cucumber and hit with a hammer, it sliced the whole cucumber with one blow.

On one trip to Sacramento for supplies, he ran into a good buy on fresh peas, loaded the car with them, and set himself the task of shelling and canning them. Shelling a carload of peas is no fun, so Phil conceived the bright idea of running them through the wringer of an old washing machine. He recalls, "As fast as we could feed the pods into the wringer, the peas would pop out one side, and the pods would go through the wringer. We lost a few peas that way, but it was a cinch."

A man who was buying one of Phil's lots at Lake Tahoe made a partial payment in walnuts and prunes: *eight hunderd pounds* of each. Mr. A canned enough prunes to last five years and gave the rest away to everyone he knew. Then a neighbor showed him how to vacuum-pack the walnuts in Mason jars, and he put up thirty cases of two-quart jars, which endured so well that eighteen years later the leftovers were still fresh.

During this period Phil was obligingly coming to the aid of anyone who requested his services without charge. A deputy real estate commissioner who drove from Sacramento to Lake Tahoe with Phil to make a report on his property, mentioned that doctors had said his infant son could not live because he was vomiting everything he ate. At Phil's suggestion they stopped off to see the baby, and as he watched, a bubble or lump the size of an olive would periodically move diagonally across the infant's abdomen: Mr. A put his fingers on the space in front of it, and it stopped, never again to reappear. Then he sent a charge of energy to the magnetic field, and the baby's parents noticed that his breathing increased in depth, his cheeks went pink, and he gave a relaxing stretch. Three months later, the father reported that the baby was gaining weight and retaining his food. Some twenty years afterward the father, by then an attorney in Oakland, told Phil that his son was healthy, normal, and happily married. Today, such a condition is diagnosed as congenital pyloric stenosis, and normally requires surgery.

Like many people in those bleak Depression years, Phil was having financial difficulties. The bank loan on the lodge he had built at Lake Tahoe was about to be foreclosed, and after trying every other available source, he went to see an old cattleman, known as a tightwad, who occasionally made loans in the vicinity of Auburn. He was a tall, lean man who had difficulty walking even with the homemade cane he had whittled out of a tree stump, and as the two men talked, Mr. East would half lean and half sit on this stump. Phil told him he would like him to buy the note and deed of trust on the lodge from the bank, and let him pay a flat rate of interest for one year, but the old man snarled, "I don't want anything to do with Lake Tahoe."

Unable to suppress a laugh, Mr. A said, "Look, you need me a hell of a lot more than I need you. You can hardly put one foot past the other."

"Yeah," the old man grunted. "I was thrown from horses and then I broke my hip, and now I have arthritis. I've been to the best doctors and they told me to go home and save my money, because they can't do anything for me."

Nodding sympathetically, Phil told him, "The distance across your yard is about a hundred and fifty feet. If you can run it in two days' time, will you cover this deal?"

Squinting, Mr. East mumbled, "You're crazy," and Phil countered, "Crazy or not, is it a deal?"

Snickering, the old man said, "On a deal like that, what have I got to lose? We'll shake on it, but I still think you're crazy. When do we start?"

"Now!" Phil replied. "When is your brithday?" Learning that it was the early part of November, he had Mr. East sit on a stump in the yard while he went to work to open his circuits. He still recalls it vividly today: "I loaded him with all the power I could deliver, realizing what was at stake. After about ten minutes I told him to get up and kick his feet. He did. 'Well,' he said, 'They don't hurt.' I told him, 'Now run,' and he ran abut a hundred feet, but one leg didn't track good, so I brought him back and gave him more energy. Then I told him, 'Go in and rest, and I'll see you here in the morning.' I was back the next morning, working with him, and pretty soon he ran the full length of his yard and back again. He just stood and laughed like a kid, bewildered. Then suddenly he said, 'When is the deadline on that foreclosure?' I said, 'Tomorrow,' and he said, 'How much did you say it was? Here, I'll make you the check. You get the hell down there and get that paper assigned to me before something happens.' "

After healing the elderly cripple, Mr. A saw his fame spread rapidly, and ranchers from the surrounding countryside would be at his door every morning, whittling and waiting, and he would take care of their ailments before starting his own day.

About this time Phil heard that a cannery in Sacramento was giving good buys on dented cans of fruit. Thanks to his Herculean efforts, he needed no more canned fruit, but it occurred to him that he might be able to buy dented cans of fish at a similar bargain price. He went to a fish cannery in Monterey and was directed to the office of the manager. The manager came limping in, complaining that doctors had not been able to repair the damage from an accident. Mr. A offered to work on it, and after the treatment the manager could not find his limp or feel the pain. They chatted a while about the man's condition, but the manager evaded all questions about the possibility of buying damaged cans of fish.

Later, on returning to his car, Phil found it so loaded with cases of canned sardines and other fish that the springs were nearly down to the axles. There was barely room for him to sit to drive, and Mr. A subsequently delivered cases to practically every friend and neighbor in the lake area, who all enjoyed a high-protein diet of sardines that winter.

One day, in the lobby of a hotel, a woman Phil knew asked him to come upstairs and "help Rae, a friend of mine who's in a bad way." Mr. A says of the incident, "When we entered the room, I found Rae in a convulsion, with a man sitting beside her whom I assumed to be her husband. While she was struggling, I leaned my ear to her chest, and it sounded like dice being shaken in a leather case. After giving her energy to release the pressure and strengthen her magnetic field, and wanting to cross-fire the lungs to drain them, I asked her to sit up. The man said, 'What did you tell that woman to do?' I said, 'I told her to sit up.'

"He said, 'Wait a minute!' And out of his pocket he drew a stethoscope. I realized then that he was a doctor, and after listening to her heart, he said, 'I don't know what you've done, but you've helped her. Proceed with your orders.' I later learned the man was her brother-in-law, a heart specialist, and that she had been on thirty-five drops of digitalis a day."

Phil's youthful marriage had long since gone on the rocks, and later he would marry Rae in order to give her constant supervision and care. Meanwhile, he continued to unravel the red tape surrounding the Lake Tahoe property, and by 1941 he not only was able to turn over the separated property to the legal heirs but also to amass substantial holdings for himself.

# CHAPTER V

## His Lifework Begins

Mr. A's inner instructions not only make it possible for him to heal, but they also advise him of courses to pursue. I ventured to ask how he receives the information, and he replied, "I listen, and they tell me."

Who are "they"?

"Why, the Powers," he said blandly. I asked whether he actually hears voices, and he responded, "I hear nothing vocally. The power is translated into words in my brain. The 'knowing' is simply put there."

Such a message came to him during the summer of 1941. He was told that on October 3 he should establish residence in Reno, Nevada, to begin his main lifework. He was to align himself with no organized group but simply to follow instructions coming from The Universal Ring of Wisdom . . . the Power of Powers.

"My instructions were that I was not to explain anything," he says of this particular period. "When people asked me questions, my answer was to be that I was not a doctor and that I didn't know anything. I was simply to be instructed, and the energies would make the corrections through me as a generator. If people became overly excited by the speed of the energy's correction, my reply was to be, 'It's crazy, isn't it?' "

Mr. A checked in at the old Golden Hotel, a real Western landmark with slot machines and an antique barroom off the lobby, where the oldtimers gathered to swap tall tales. When an attorney advised him that in order to establish legal residence he would have to have a Nevada citizen witness the fact that he had been seen at least once every twenty-four hours for six weeks, Phil appointed a hotel bellboy as witness.

Now he was ready for action, but for two days while awating further instructions he restlessly strolled the casinos, took in the movies, and sat in the lobby. On the third morning he was loafing near the hotel desk when Elmo, one of the bellboys, came up and said, "I've been looking all over for a stretcher and can't find one anywhere. The hotel engineer is downstairs lying on his back and can't move. This isn't the first time we've had to pack him off to the hospital for this condition."

"Why are you telling me?" Phil asked curiously.

"I don't know," Elmo answered. "Just seems like I should. But you're a subdivider out at Lake Tahoe, aren't you? What could you do in a case like this?"

Mr. A followed the boy downstairs and saw the hotel's co-managers standing over a man lying on the floor. Reaching down, Phil sent a charge of energy through him, and almost immediately he was on his feet. Mystified, one of the managers asked Phil if he could do something to help his heart condition, which prevented him from working more than an hour or two a day. A few blasts of the magical energy, and he was back at work full time.

Later that day, walking along the street, Mr. A felt the handle of a cane hooking his arm and heard an old man say, "I'm Dr. Addington. Aren't you the fellow who used to be with Dr. Hill in the Bay Area? I heard you were in town, and I've been looking for you. What can you do for this stroke paralysis?" Phil looked him over, observing that he dragged one leg, walked with a crutch and a cane, and was unable to lift one arm.

"Let's go to my room," Phil said, "and see what the energy can do for you." Immediately after receiving the charge, the old doctor began swinging his arm over his head and kicking with his bad leg.

"I couldn't do any of these things before coming up here," the old man exulted, and without thinking began walking effortlessly around the room. Suddenly remembering, he asked with a chuckle, "What am I going to do with this crutch?" Then he walked out of the hotel carrying the crutch and swinging his cane, and because he had been health officer in Reno for ten years, the news of his "miraculous healing" traveled fast.

The next morning a woman on two crutches stopped Mr. A in the hotel lobby, saying that Dr. Addington had told her, "If you can find Phil A, you won't need your crutches any longer." Six months earlier she had fractured a leg but still could not bear the pressure and pain of standing or walking. Phil was late for an appointment, and the lobby provided little privacy, but he told her to step behind the slot machines. As soon as the energy was sent from her hip down through her leg, she pronounced the pain nonexistent and went delightfully off down the street carrying the crutches under her arm.

Dr. Addington next sent Phil a state Senator who had been forced to retire because of crippling arthritis. He came in snarling with pain, but after a few treatments in which Phil distributed the energy, he said he felt like a new man. Shortly afterward he ran and was reelected to the Senate.

Next Dr. Addington called Phil, saying, "This evening I want to bring in one of my worst heart cases. I want to check her out while you do whatever it is you do." After dinner Dr. and Mrs. Addington arrived with the woman, and as Phil started to work on her energy field, the old doctor exclaimed, "Wait, I want to see how long this will take for correction," and pulled out his pocket watch. The doctor listened to her erratic heartbeat, before Phil began energizing her field. Then he exclaimed, "This heart is normal now! And it took exactly two and a half minutes to do it."

Phil treated a number of cases that week in Reno, before making a quick trip to Lake Tahoe to take care of some business. When he returned the next morning, the hotel lobby was thronged with people, and he asked a bystander if there was a convention in town. "No, there's a miracle man staying at the hotel," the man replied, "and we're all waiting to see him."

Mr. A wanted to see the miracle man, too, so he joined the curious throng, but when nothing had happened after a couple of hours he spotted Jimmy, the bellboy who had to vouch for his daily presence, and asked, "What's this about a miracle man staying in the hotel?"

Jimmy flashed a quizzical look. "Don't you know that they're looking for *you?*"

Shocked, Phil said, "Look, don't you dare say anything about it. I'm getting out of here."

"Well, you gotta be back within twenty-four hours," Jimmy replied with a broad grin.

Mr. A jumped into his car and headed for Carson City, laughing to himself all the way. What a crazy thing to have happen! He a miracle man! That was crazy! But rather than forfeit his terms for legal residence he had to head back for Reno, and when he entered the hotel, the district attorney's right-hand man said, "The DA wants you."

"OK," Phil said. "Let's go."

At his office, the district attorney demanded, "What in the hell are you doing around here, stirring up Reno? Why don't you stay up at Lake Tahoe where you belong?"

"I have to be here for a year," Phil replied, thinking of his inner instructions.

The district attorney asked Phil how much money he had made from his healing work, and on learning he had never yet charged for it, the DA said, "Well, you're in the clear there, but I do resent your disturbing my sleep. People are calling at all hours wanting me to put them in touch with you."

The next morning the hotel lobby was crowded with ailing people, and Phil began working on them in his own room, one after another, all day. Toward evening the deputy telephoned to say, "The DA wants to see you again."

At his office the district attorney greeted Mr. A: "What do you call yourself?"

"You name it," he replied with a shrug.

"There was only one other person I ever heard about who could perform miracles like that," the DA muttered under his breath. Then he said, "I have to do something about you."

Grinning, Phil suggested, "Why don't you give me a letter telling me I'm not allowed to help these people? That way I'll get some rest."

"Give you a letter, hell!" he snapped. "I have orders from the Governor of Nevada on down to get you licensed so you can practice. They apparently think you're needed here. I've been doing a lot of checking, looking for a way to manage this, and I think I have it. There's a statute on the books whereby any four state, county, or city officials can meet together and pass any emergency measure they see fit. I'll see about it in the morning."

By noon the state Senator was in Phil's room waving a piece of paper. "You've got your license," he said. "Here it is." Mr. A thanked him and asked how much he owed as a fee. "Nothing," he bellowed. "Now get to work."

The following morning a policeman who had been injured while making an arrest came to see Phil, complaining that he was "aching from head to foot." Within ten minutes he could not locate a single sore spot, and the police department promptly adopted Phil, giving him a windshield sticker reading DOCTOR'S EMERGENCY CAR, so that he could get where he needed to go in a hurry, and the police made good use of his services. At movies, casinos, or restaurants, they would summon him with "Dr. A, please report to the front of the building," and a squad car would be waiting to rush him to the scene of an accident or other emergency.

In June of 1942 he made a brief trip to Los Angeles, where at the request of one of his Reno patients, he saw her cousin who was paralyzed from the neck down. After the energy charge had been sent through her, another woman in the room became so excited at the beneficial results that she said, "I'm an osteopath and I'm kidnapping you. You're coming with me." Not stopping for a yes or no, she began whisking him around Hollywood and Beverly Hills, taking him to the homes of the celebrities who were her regular clients. A famous motion picture producer was so pleased with the results of Phil's treatments that he urged him to move there and "treat the actors and actresses who go to pieces on the set from nervous disorders while we're filming." He offered a handsome retainer, and although Mr. A's inner orders were that he remain for a full year in Reno, he did agree to apply for a city license to practice in Los Angeles.

After making application, he was asked to appear before the police commission of twelve men, a routine procedure except that a doctor who was an investigator for the local medical society argued against granting the license to a "quack." One of the officials pointed to a partially paralyzed man who was laboriously sweeping the floor and said, "We all know he's had a stroke and can't raise one arm. Let's see if Mr. A can help him."

Realizing that he was being deliberately tested, Phil generated a charge of energy below the crippled man's shoulder, saying, "Now can you raise your arm?" The cripple's arm shot up over his head, and

Mr. A breathed a sigh of relief. There was very little conversation after that, and in a few minutes the police commissioner told him to go upstairs and pick up his license. The head of the license bureau had apparently been briefed by telephone, because he asked eagerly, "Will you help two of the girls here in the office while I'm getting your license ready?" With no other privacy available, Phil treated each of them behind the filing cabinets, and when they pronounced the pain in their aching backs gone, the bureau chief handed over the license.

Back in Reno, the state Senator brought a friend who complained of constant pain from arthritis throughout his body. Scarcely able to walk, he could not raise either arm, but the Senator said, "Phil, I know you can help him." After a single session, the man was able to put on his coat without assistance or pain, and Mr. A's fame continued to spread. The Chairman of the Board of Supervisors came from San Francisco for energy, telling Mr. A that he suffered from arthritis and a heart condition, and after being helped he urged Phil to come there to practice.

Mr. A had now completed his year in Reno, and the inner instructions gave him a choice of Los Angeles or San Francisco as his next residence. Without hesitation he chose San Francisco, because friends had advised him that it would be "the toughest place to try anything new and different," and the challenge appealed to him. When he said his good-byes to his Reno friends, the county clerk was so grateful for all Mr. A had done for him and his family that he gave him an unsolicited letter of recommendation, which he still has.

On his arrival in San Francisco the Chairman of the Board of Supervisors introduced Phil to the head of the city's Health Department and a license for magnetic treatments was promptly issued. "We know what you can do," the health official said. "We just want to know where you are when we need you." Since the license now permitted him to charge a fee for his services, he could at last afford to devote full time to helping suffering humanity.

# CHAPTER VI

# The War Years

It was December of 1942 when Mr. A rented office space on San Francisco's Market Street. Considerable time was required to redecorate and furnish the quarters, and during this waiting period he treated an official in charge of shipping for Oakland's Ninth Avenue Pier, who for years had been suffering from diabetes. The man was so pleased with the progress he was making under Phil's skilled hands that they became good friends, and, since the war was raging on two fronts, the shipper often cited the strategic moves which "noted authorities" had predicted would be made during World War II.

"As he talked," Phil recalls, "I would get corrections on what he said from The Ring and would then tell him the exact dates when certain events would transpire. These were usually six to eight weeks in advance, and included such data as when Rommel would cross the desert and how far he would go, the date we would land our troops in France, and the date Mussolini's control would suddenly disintegrate in Italy. When I called these future events, the official offered to bet me that they would happen instead like his 'noted authorities' said, but since I invariably won, he laughingly refused to bet with me anymore and accused me of having inside information."

Mr. A was now engaged to marry Rae, who persuaded him to call on a friend who'd been born a cripple. "One of her legs has had to be amputated," Rae said, "and the other is only partially developed. Now she has developed such severe arthritis that she can't turn her head, and she can scarcely operate her wheelchair anymore." Phil obligingly went to see her, and he says that the energies soon made it possible for her to turn her head normally, rotate her shoulders without pain, and use her wheelchair with ease. The woman was so elated that she urged Mr. A to see Mrs. Wade, a friend of hers confined to bed with a severe heart condition. Mrs. Wade also telephoned to request his services, and when he called at her home he was admitted by her husband, who greeted Phil courteously but said, "Anything to keep my wife happy," as if to let him know he had no faith in such shenanigans. The impeccably dressed gentleman then used a crutch to hobble ahead of Mr. A to his wife's room.

Phil set to work as usual, and after receiving the charge of energy through her lower abdomen, Mrs. Wade exclaimed, "Oh, that elephant is off my chest. My lungs have no bottom! My feet are tingling and warm, as they haven't been for years." She urged Phil to return, and during each session Mr. Wade would sit beside the bed, extolling the virtues of his wonderful doctors. He said he had recently undergone surgery for phlebitis, and because his leg and ankle were still severely swollen, it would be necessary for him to use a crutch for some time.

Toward the end of the week, as Phil was completing his treatment of Mrs. Wade, he playfully reached over and generated a crosscurrent of energy through Mr. Wade's ankle, saying, "Here, see what this does for you." The next day the man greeted Mr. A at the door without his crutch. His ankle had returned to normal size, and when the treatment of his wife was finished, the fastidious old gentleman told Phil, "I want you to continue coming every day, because I also want the energy from you."

Mr. A explained that he would not be able to return, because his office would be opening Monday, but that he and Mrs. Wade could come to see him there if they wished to continue. The proud old man said he couldn't consider coming to an office where other clients were waiting their turn, and Phil, bidding them a cheery good-bye, said it was entirely up to them. Monday morning, among the first to arrive in his new office were Mr. and Mrs. Wade. "I also have uremic poisoning," the chastened gentleman confided, "and I've been seeing a specialist for it. Can you do anything for that?"

"I can't answer that," Mr. A replied. "We'll just give you the energy and see what happens."

After the third session, Mr. Wade charged into the office, exclaiming, "The doctor is amazed with the change in my condition. After making new tests, he and the specialist tell me that I now have the kidneys of a twenty-year-old. I didn't tell them I was seeing you, so they're completely mystified. They said there's no longer any evidence of uremia or phlebitis, but they don't know why."

Mr. A said that he was glad to hear it, and that Mr. Wade would not need to return for further treatments, but the nearly eighty-year-old man bellowed, "Not return! Listen, boy, I'm going to take a charge of energy every week from now on. Your fees are pretty cheap life insurance, you know."

Very much the distinguished banker, always impeccably turned out, with shirt fronts starched, Mr. Wade continued to come to Phil's office, along with his wife, every week for the next fourteen years. At ninety-four he was still driving his own car, appraising property, and making loans on land in the Berkeley Hills. Then one day, carrying a parakeet cage down the steps to his garage without holding onto the banister, he fell head first down the full length of stairs, crushing the cage against the wall with his head. He was hospitalized with a brain concussion, from which he died before he could see Phil, but amazed doctors noted that not a single bone was broken. Mr. A says that the energy he sends through patients is notable for keeping bones young and flexible.

During this same period of years, the woman in the wheelchair who had originally asked Mr. A to see the Wades was also continuing to take energy treatments, but after her ninety-seventh birthday she decided to stop the sessions, "because I'm afraid I'll outlive my financial resources."

Another of Phil's early San Francisco clients was a stockbroker from a leading brokerage firm, who complained of the asthma that kept him awake nights, and said he was scheduled for a prostate operation. After several charges of the mysterious energy, he told Mr. A that his doctor had canceled the surgery as unnecessary, and that he was sleeping like a child. Then he sent in his wife, also an insomniac, who said that the doctors had given her less than a year to live, because of a rare anemic condition. After receiving her first charge of energy, she bluntly told Mr. A, "This is the silliest thing I've ever encountered. I wouldn't be here except for my husband's insistence, and I didn't feel a thing when you supposedly treated me."

A few days later she returned, confessing that she had enjoyed her first full night's sleep in many years after the treatment, and said, "I don't know what that silly thing that you do does, but it works, so keep doing it." The stockbroker and his wife continued taking energy periodically for a while; then Mr. A lost track of them. When the broker was eighty-five years old, and his wife a year younger, he sought Phil out again, saying he had been hospitalized in intensive care for a severe heart condition and would like to resume treatments. To this day they still come in periodically for charges of the revitalizing energy.

The broker sent Mr. A a number of other clients, including Mrs. Robeson, a cripple who required two people, plus braces, a crutch and cane, to help her walk. As he first began generating energy to each side of her crippled knee, she cried out, "Ohhhh, you're hurting me. I'll wrap my cane around your neck," but when shortly afterward she began walking without assistance, she became one of his most ardent supporters.

Among his first clients in the new office was a middle-aged nurse who complained of exhaustion and low metabolism, but when her metabolism returned to normal after a few treatments she began sending in her own medical patients, many of whom held high executive positions in the Bay Area. One had retired two years earlier as vice-president of General Motors, owing to a paralyzing stroke, but after a few treatments he again had full use of his incapacitated arm and leg. Later, while vacationing at Camel Back Inn near Phoenix, he developed painful hemorrhoids and flew back to San Francisco to see Mr. A.

"Hemorrhoids are mad bumps," Phil told him. "You must have gotten very angry to cause such an aggravated case." Surprised, he admitted he had, but after receiving the energy from Phil his hemorrhoids disappeared, and he flew back to rejoin his wife in Arizona.

Another referral was a young Army officer who, while on a tour of duty in the Pacific, had contracted "jungle feet." His feet and lower legs were covered with weeping, reddened ulcers, and despite the attention of Army doctors familiar with the condition, there had been no improvement. After Phil distributed the energy through his legs and feet, the ulcers began to subside, and a few days later he demonstrated that the condition had entirely disappeared. Later, after his honorable discharge from the Armed Forces, he began dropping by to chat with Phil and ask his advice about business matters. On one such occasion he confided that although they very much wanted children, his wife had been unable to pass the second or third month of pregnancy without miscarrying. "Can you do anything about this kind of condition?" he asked hopefully.

Shrugging his husky shoulders, Mr. A replied, "The next time that she's about six weeks along, bring her in and we'll see what the energy can do for her." Before long she came to his office, and returned regularly for monthly charges of the energy until her full-term baby was born. Three years later, the veteran told Phil that his wife was again having miscarriages, so he sent her in for another series of treatments, and this pregnancy also produced a healthy baby.

Some time elapsed before Phil saw the couple again. Then the husband came in to say that the birth of their third child was overdue, and the family doctor had told him to bring his wife into the hospital that evening for a Caesarian section the next morning. Phil, who had an office full of patients, replied, "As soon as I get through here, I'll go to your house with you." There he gave the wife a charge of energy to relax the tension and pressure, and the next morning the jubilant husband called to say that by the time he returned to the house after driving Phil home, his wife was in labor, and he rushed her to the hospital for a normal delivery. Now, twenty-eight years later, the man still comes for energy recharges four or five times a year, "just to keep myself in shape."

One day a group from Los Altos Hills, some of whom had been Phil's patients, came to the office to ask him about a rare and so-called incurable condition which had a long medical name unfamiliar to him. "A friend of ours has a five-year-old boy who suffers from this condition," the spokesman said, "and he has been written up in the medical journals as quite a rarity. The articles report that children with this ailment mature prematurely, but do not live beyond the age of six. Can you do anything for it?"

"How do I know until the boy is in front of me?" Phil asked quietly.

When the parents brought in the boy, his body resembled a dwarf's, with a protruding belly, although emotionally he appeared wise beyond his years. Phil bent his ear to the child's chest, listened to the vibrations, and received his inner instructions. Then he went to work on his magnetic field, and within minutes the expanded liver and belly began to assume a normal appearance, the boy took the first deep breath he had seemingly drawn since birth, and his body began drawing energy from the lungs. The elated parents later reported to Mr. A that the child specialist who had been treating the youngster was "very proud" of the results of his prescribed diet, until they told him about the treatment from Mr. A. Then, they said, he was furious.

A month or so later an aunt again brought the boy to Mr. A, reporting that his testicles had not yet descended. She said the child's doctor told them he usually operated for such a condition after the age of six, but that owing to his ailment, the operation would not be indicated in this case. Mr. A set to work distributing the energy through the nerves controlling the testicles. They descended immediately into the scrotum.

Many years later a member of the group who had originally interested him in the unusual case reported that the boy had matured normally, both mentally and physically, had completed school and was now married.

The Bay Area was full of characters in those days, and two of the most colorful were Captain and Mrs. Quay, English expatriates who lived on a four-mast sailing ship perched on concrete piers in the Sausalito

Harbor. The captain had commanded a British ship during the First World War, but was now an antique dealer and interior decorator. His wife, a registered nurse, told Mr. A that for many years she had been in constant pain from arthritis. After a few charges of energy she wrote to Phil's wife, "He has given me a new lease on life!" Ten years later, during which time she had received periodic charges of the energy, she wrote again, saying, "I am still free of all arthritic pains and am enjoying life in my eighties."

The Quays sent many people to Mr. A, among them a dentist who had been forced to relinquish a busy practice and retire to a small town near Santa Cruz, because of a serious heart condition. As Mr. A describes this case, "When the energy was first generated through his magnetic field, opening the blockage, he momentarily passed out. Then, to his surprise, he found he could breathe deeply for the first time in years. He took energy recharges until he was satisfied his heart was in shape. Then he not only resumed his dental practice but sent in many relatives to receive the energy. About twenty years later, he developed an enlarged nodule in his right breast. From his medical experience he realized its seriousness and the usual consequences of a tumor in the male breast, so he resigned himself to an early death. The growth continued to enlarge rapidly, and one day while he was cleaning my teeth, he mentioned it to me for the first time. I told him to wish me luck, and then began cross-firing the energy from several directions, especially from the right calf of the leg, as my inner instructions directed, and the mass started to diminish before our eyes. When the tension was completely released, there was no trace of the breast mass, and the other day he told me that there had never been any recurrence of it during the intervening years."

Many of Phil's early patients in San Francisco were nurses, who were so delighted with the seeming miracles he effected with their maladies that they spread the word among their patients. Some brought ailing children, and a nurse who worked closely with Mr. A in those years said it was fascinating to watch the almost totally incapacitated spastic children, blue babies, and rheumatic fever cases respond to the treatments, holding up their heads for the first time, walking and playing.

About six weeks after Mr. A opened his office on Market Street, an official of the Mare Island Naval Shipyard near Vallejo came in and, after experiencing Phil's treatment, exclaimed, "Listen, we need your help desperately in Vallejo. We have a war raging on two fronts, and many of our most vitally needed employees at the shipyard miss work because of a variety of ailments. It's critical to the war effort to get them back on the job as soon as possible. Will you help?"

Mr. A, who was too old for active duty during World War II, agreed to make trips to Vallejo for ten weeks. He would crowd all his San Francisco patients into the morning hours, then jump into his car and drive the forty miles to Vallejo. Mrs. Reed, one of his elderly patients, offered her old-fashioned house in Vallejo for Phil's work, and when she saw the hordes of patients pulling into the alley behind her house, she began dividing them into two categories: "bedroom people and alley people." The latter was not a term of opprobrium. She was simply referring to those who were too lame or ill to enter the house, so Mr. A would go out to their cars to generate the energy to them.

Mrs. Reed was a buxom, motherly type who clucked over the patients and became highly excited as she saw the seeming miracles being wrought on her premises. Soon her concern became personal; her brother owned a ranch in Lake County, and while he was unharnessing a team of horses they became frightened and dragged him several hundred feet, before slamming him against a gate post. He had already been suffering so acutely with heart trouble that he needed help to get out of bed, and now he was seriously injured. But he was a tough old rancher with a "show me" attitude, and not until the accident was Mrs. Reed able to persuade him to try a treatment from Phil. After the first session, he was able to get on his feet by himself. Two days later, while sitting in the kitchen awaiting his turn for Phil's ministrations, he fell off the chair, and Mrs. Reed banged on the door where Mr. A was treating another patient.

"Hurry, please," she urged. "Edgar has fallen off the chair and won't move." Darting into the kitchen, Mr. A put his ear to the old rancher's chest and could hear nothing. Hastily, with a hand on each side of his chest, he sent the energy charging through him. Then, leaving his left hand on the man's chest, he moved his right hand to his magnetic field while continuing to generate the energy. The old rancher began to stir, and then to vomit, muttering that he was so sick to his stomach he didn't want to live. Ten minutes later, however, he was on his feet and walking around the kitchen. Mr. A returned to the patient he had been working on, who was not in much better shape, and a week later the rancher was back at work tending the cattle and chickens.

By now Mr. A's afternoon and evening sessions in Vallejo had run well beyond the agreed-upon ten weeks, but there seemed no chance of breaking away. Daily the house swarmed with ailing people, not only from the shipyard but also from Vallejo and as far north as Lake County. Mr. A's San Francisco patients were pleading for his full-time services, and letters from Reno nearly broke his heart. "Why did you leave us?" old friends were writing. "Didn't we treat you right? We need you, too."

One evening in Vallejo, as a favor to a friend, he went to see a bedridden man before returning to San Francisco for the night. Doctors had told the patient that he could not live, and Attorney Tim O'Grady was there to draw his last will and testament. He watched while Phil went to work on his client, and then said, "I've heard about you. O'Grady's my name. That head printer at the shipyard, that you cured of Buerger's disease, happens to be my father-in-law. I'm crippled myself, since childhood, and I've been in constant pain following an operation to correct the deformity. Do you think at this late stage you could do anything for me?"

Phil obligingly pumped the energy into him, and after five minutes the attorney was able to straighten up, and even lift his foot onto a chair for the first time since childhood. The next day he sent his wife to Mrs. Reed's house for treatment, and the merry little woman told Mr. A that the evening before her husband had come home standing erect and swinging his bad leg around. When she questioned him about the sudden change for the better, he replied, "I'll tell you what happened, but if you laugh I'll sock you one."

The next time Attorney O'Grady came in for treatment, he said, "Phil, I almost wish that you would get into trouble so that I could represent you, and show you how good I am."

Instead of chuckling at Tim's sally, Mr. A replied soberly, "You know, Tim, that is going to happen very soon."

O'Grady gave him a quizzical look, but Mr. A said no more. His inner instructions had already told him he would have to be arrested and acquitted, in order to carry forward his lifework, and he sensed the testing time was very near.

# CHAPTER VII

## The Medical Trial

Mr. A's inner instructions had been explicit. A court trial was essential to his continuing work as an instrument of the Powers, and he was not to resist arrest. The day before the summons, he had finished his weekly stint in Vallejo and was ready to drive home to San Francisco when he had a mental flash: "Wait for him."

Within ten minutes a tall man arrived, asking, "Is Doctor A here?" Without responding, Phil waved him into the bedroom where he worked on Vallejo patients. "I have a very bad heart condition," the stranger said, and began to outline the usual symptoms.

Phil put his ear to the man's chest, and later told me, "My intuition and inner feelings did not indicate the condition he had described, only the emotion of being there to arrest me. I was so amused that I thought, 'As long as I'm in for it, I may as well make this good,' so I gave him a good charge of energy in the ribs, which momentarily knocked him out. In a moment he came to and began asking what had happened. Half babbling, he asked, 'Is that all?' and I laughingly said, 'Isn't that enough?'

"Then he began writing out a check, asking to

whom it should be made payable, and when he handed it to me, I said, 'I'll never cash this check. It isn't any good anyway.' Then he wanted to know how many more treatments he would need to 'clean up my condition,' and I replied that he didn't need any more, but he asked, 'Will you be here tomorrow?' Knowing that tomorrow would be the day of my arrest, I prepared for it by hiding five one-hundred-dollar bills in a separate part of my clothing, and putting a few unsolicited testimonial letters in my pocket. I knew that my pockets would be searched."

The next afternoon Phil was generating energy to the first of his waiting patients in Vallejo when the tall man arrived with a constable, who said, "You're under arrest," and started to read the warrant. Phil told him that was unnecessary, but he continued on to the last period. Then the special agent of the California State Board of Medical Examiners, who had experienced Phil's blast of energy the previous day, cut to shreds the pillow on which Mr. A had been sitting and turned both of their chairs upside down to examine them for hidden electrical wires. While Mrs. Reed angrily gave him a piece of her mind for ruining one of her pillows, the agent continued searching the room, but all he could find was a card with Phil's name printed on it. He took the name and address of the man on whom Mr. A had been working, and then asked the identities of the nine women in the waiting room. Until then, the ladies had been tranquilly waiting their turn, knitting and chatting, but as soon as the agent began asking them questions about Phil, they behaved like the mythological Furies, refusing to speak except to say that it was none of his business.

For a few minutes Mr. A good-humoredly watched the fur fly and then said with a laugh, "Look, ladies, this poor fellow is only doing his job. This is the way he makes his living, so give him the information he wants, including your names and addresses." Aware that the prosecution would subpoena the man and nine women, Phil knew that he could have no better witnesses at his trial.

En route to the police station, the constable cleared his throat a few times before saying, "Mr. A, you are very well liked by Vallejo. The people seem to think highly of you. I just don't understand this procedure." At the station Phil posed for a mug shot, but before the officials could fingerprint him the medical agent eagerly began examining his fingers.

"What are you looking for, hidden wires?" the constable asked sarcastically, and the agent said, "I just wanted to make sure there were no surgery marks."

Next they emptied Mr. A's pockets, and the medical agent eagerly grabbed the testimonial letters and gas-rationing tickets, while the constable sealed his loose change and other items in an official envelope. Then they led him to a cell, but Phil said, "I'm not going in there."

"What makes you think you aren't?" the agent snapped. "You don't have any bail money on you."

With a flip of his wrist, Mr. A produced the hidden five hundred dollars, saying, "Write me out a receipt. I have to get back to work." The medical agent seemed as stunned as if Phil had materialized the money out of thin air, but the constable said with a half-grin, "Write him out a receipt. I'll get his belongings."

The agent made no move to return the letters and ration books, and was so nervous in writing out the receipt that he made it for five dollars instead of five hundred. The constable had to redo it. Phil was now free to leave on bail, but instead he asked permission to call a lawyer, and when they heard him address Tim O'Grady on the telephone, the agent muttered irately, "He's the best."

Soon Tim arrived, and when he learned the agent had retained the letters and ration books, he demanded a receipt, which was quickly produced. Then the lawyer asked, "Where do we go from here?"

"I'm going back to work," Mr. A replied. "I have an office full of people."

"We'll arrest you again then." The agent glowered, but Tim O'Grady advised him not to molest Mr. A further until the trial, and Phil continued to practice. A few days after the arrest, he received a letter ordering him to appear at the rationing board headquarters in San Francisco, where the medical agent had filed a complaint charging that his extra gas rations were illegal. Phil readily appeared, and the records showed that the civilian executives of Mare Island Naval Shipyard had requested one book in order to enable Mr. A to make the daily trips to Vallejo. The other was his regular one, for occasional trips to Lake Tahoe to oversee his property there. The officials showed Phil letters from several of the Mare Island executives, highly praising his work in keeping essential employees on the job. Then the chairman said laughingly, "What the hell! It's getting good when the medical association wants us to fight their battles for them. They must not have much of a case. Sorry we troubled you

108

to come in here. Everything's in order. Good-bye and good luck."

The medical agent smeared Phil in California newspapers, claiming he had been "driven out of Reno," and that he was a charlatan. As a consequence, the press was well represented at the arraignment, when the judge set a time and place for the trial to determine whether Mr. A had violated the Fair Trades Act under which the California Medical Association operated. Immediately after the hearing, Tim O'Grady took advantage of the large newspaper turnout to question the medical agent about his accusations.

Holding out a stack of testimonials, he asked, "Would you like to see these letters? Here is one from the county clerk of Washoe County, Nevada, pertaining to our friend and showing that Reno was very fond of him." (I have seen the original of this letter, written December 1, 1942, on the official stationery of the county clerk and signed by him, which reads: "To whom it may concern. Mr. A [real name is actually used] has been working in Reno for about a year. He effected outstanding cures immediately when he first started in Reno, which resulted in bringing to him a large practice. A great number of people in Reno praised his results by keeping him busy. He has corrected my son-in-law from a critical heart condition which enabled him to return to his work after the second treatment, which was eleven months ago, and he has been employed at manual labor and working ten hours a day since. Prior to the treatment he was unable to do a day's work for eight months, and he was under a physician's care for several years. Last June [Mr. A] was also successful in treating my wife and myself for an illness and the results were prompt. I know many people in Reno join with me in recommending him for the uncanny results he has accomplished while doctoring here, and we are all grateful for the same.")

"Would you like to see the license that Reno gave him to practice?" O'Grady homed in on the medical agent in front of the reporters. "Now I ask you, does this look like he was driven out of Reno, as you stated to the press?" The agent turned on his heel and left.

A few days later, at the request of some of the reporters, Phil worked on a large group of them who were suffering from a variety of ailments including stiff joints, painful arthritis, emphysema, hypertension, and migraine headaches. At the end of the session, relieved of their aches and tensions, they said in effect, "We were intending to have fun with you, but instead we've received a lot of help. We're with you now. Good luck!"

Attorney O'Grady, hearing afterward about the healing session, told Phil that he would never have permitted it, had he known in advance, but he added with a grin, "I'm glad you went, because from the reports I'm getting, you did quite a job. They all loved you.

"Incidentally," O'Grady continued, "I can't get any work done, with these disciples of yours descending on my office, questioning me to see if I'm capable of getting you out of this, and volunteering to testify for you. Unfortunately, most of them are too good to use, like the gal from Lake County yesterday who stated that when you touched her neck two months ago, she swallowed her goiter and hasn't had it since.

She wanted to testify on this in court, but I told her we'd never get the jury to believe it."

The attorney shook his head and then roared with laughter. "You really have me on the spot, and to think I asked for this! You cured my father-in-law, you eliminated my mother's arthritic hip pains so she can get around normally. You've made a new man out of me, and my wife's allergies which had bothered her most of her life are gone. Now, you so-and-so, I have to get you out of this or I won't be able to go home nights."

During the waiting period before the trial, attorney friends in Sacramento told Phil the California Medical Association had demanded his arrest but had been holding off in hope that some of his patients would die, so that they would have a real case against him. Fortunately none did, and Mr. A says of that period, "The Powers were really with me! No one will ever know how many times I was very concerned, waiting until the energy took over. Many of the people who were brought to me should never have been moved out of their beds at home. They were all ages, and they had all ailments. I would energize them through the power given me and send them back to their own doctors, thinking that the doctors would be happy with their improvement. Instead, they wanted to prosecute."

Shortly before the opening of the trial, O'Grady told Mr. A, "Boy, do you rate! They're sending Ken Masters to head the prosecution team. He's their ace boy out of the attorney general's office, and is medically trained. He'll be assisted by the local district attorney."

Phil's longtime attorney friend, Bill Shelton, was working with O'Grady on the case, and while driving from San Francisco to Vallejo for the opening day of the trial, Shelton said, "I've searched every bit of evidence available, and read up on the transcripts of similar trials. I've come to the conclusion that with the Medical Association against you, you have as much chance as a snowball in hell. Much as I hate to tell you this, I think you ought to know."

Unperturbed, because he was listening to inner guidance more than to his attorneys, Mr. A asked, "You have the list I gave you of the direct questions I want you to ask me?" At his nod, Phil continued, "I want you to use the same manner and expression as if you were prosecuting instead of defending me. I'm hoping this will give us a chance for me to make an open demonstration of my work in court, although I feel the prosecutor is too intelligent to give me the opportunity."

"I never cease to be amazed at the way nothing bothers you," Shelton exclaimed. "Aren't you at all worried?"

"I haven't really thought much about it," Phil replied honestly. "I just figure this way: If the Powers want me to continue this work, they will handle it. I'm not on trial. I feel that they are. I've proved I can make a good living in several other fields, before they told me to do this work. If I'm supposed to continue, the Powers will take care of it."

So much interest had been generated by the press that the trial had to be moved from the regular courtroom to the large Assembly Hall, and after the all-female jury was selected, Ken Masters, attorney for the state, made clear the prosecution did not question what Mr. A could do for people and was not in any way challenging the benefits that his patients received from his treatments. (This, of course, was to avoid introduction of the testimonials and witnesses who would tell of his healings.) The question at issue, Masters said, was whether he was practicing medicine without a proper license from the State Medical Board, and accepting money for his services.

The first witness produced by the state was the man on whom Phil was working when he was arrested. The witness stated that, before he came to Mr. A, his legs and arms had been partially paralyzed so that he could scarcely move them; but the only thing the prosecutor wanted to know was, "How much have you paid him for this series of treatments?"

"About two hundred dollars," the witness replied, and the prosecutor looked triumphantly at the jury.

On cross-examination, Phil's attorney asked where the man had been treated for that same condition before consulting Mr. A, and he named the Mayo Clinic, the University of California and Stanford hospitals, several other hospitals throughout the country, and some private doctors.

"Did you get much help from those previous treatments?" O'Grady asked, and the man replied, "No, not a bit of help." O'Grady next asked how much he paid for the medical treatments in hospitals and private offices, and the witness gave a breakdown on each, which totaled several thousand dollars. It was

O'Grady's turn to look at the jury. Then he continued, "When this man who is on trial generated energy to you, did you get any help?"

"I got immediate help," he replied, "and I am now able to work and operate my own business again."

And so it went throughout the trial, which frequently crowded the war from the banner headlines. The prosecution questioned each witness about what Mr. A did and said before and after his treatments. Each gave the honest response that Phil first put his ear to the patient's chest, and when the patient asked what he thought was the cause of his condition, Mr. A replied, "I'm not a doctor, and I don't know anything. Do you want me to generate energy to you?" A titter swept the room when a few witnesses quoted Phil as having replied, "I don't know anything. I'm just a little boy stuttering, stumbling, and buzzing." Buzzing is Phil's favorite word for the energy charge.

Then the medical agent took the stand and testified for the prosecution. Under defense questioning, Phil's attorney suggested that Mr. A show the court how he had worked on the agent. Mr. A started forward with alacrity, but the witness attempted to leave the stand while prosecutors shouted "objection," and the courtroom rocked with laughter. Thereafter, whenever the agent looked in a door of the courtroom, members of the audience would hiss him.

The state subpoenaed the nine women patients who were in the waiting room on the day of his arrest, but after using only two or three they excused the remainder, realizing that Mr. A could not have selected more eloquent witnesses in his own defense. But they refused to go home and begged O'Grady to use them in Phil's behalf. One subsequently testified that when she first came to Mr. A she could shuffle her feet only four or five inches at a time, using a crutch and cane, with two people assisting her on either side. The prosecutor objected and refused to let her tell what the treatments had done for her, but she retorted, "Well, if you ever lock him up, you lock me in the same cell, because you can't take him away from me."

More objections from the prosecution, and she was excused from the stand, but as she effortlessly stepped down she paused at the clerk's desk and swung one leg over it, winking at the jury as she sailed out of the room unassisted. The reporters loved it, and news stories referred to her as "the witty one."

The prosecution finally managed to produce a witness who seemed critical of Mr. A. She was an elderly woman with arthritis, who testified that when she went for her first treatment, Phil put his head to her chest and said, "Oh, it's down here." She asked what was down there, but he replied, "I don't know anything." Then he put his hand on her knee, and it hurt. "He really hurt you?" the prosecutor pressed, and she replied, "Well, at the time."

Under continued questioning, she admitted that she went ten times to see Mr. A, and "at first he really helped me, but after the eighth time I couldn't feel it anymore, so I decided that he couldn't do me any more good." This remark drew derisive laughter from Phil's patients in the courtroom, who were aware that the more the energy builds up in a person, the less he feels the vibration. "Your witness," the prosecutor said triumphantly.

Tim O'Grady began cross-examination. "You said

115

that when this man worked with you, he hurt you. You gestured as though he had dug in with his fingers. Were there any marks or bruises on your knee?"

"I was sure I would be all black and blue," she began, "but I couldn't find a mark."

"I understand that your legs worked better after you received the energy?"

"Yes," she replied meekly.

"And did they continue to work better?"

"Yes."

O'Grady asked where she lived, and on learning that it was seventeen miles from Vallejo, he asked her how she had come to the trial. She reluctantly conceded that the medical agent had brought her, and Tim O'Grady, with a flash of Irish humor, said, "Oh, the investigator for the medical association kindly went to your home and got you and brought you here in his car to testify! No further questions."

The defense then took over and after a day and a half of hearing witnesses try to tell the court how greatly they had benefited from Mr. A's treatments, while the prosecutor shouted "Objection," Phil whispered, "Tim, how about it? Shall I take it from here?"

"You mean you're ready to take the stand?" O'Grady asked, and as Phil headed for the witness stand pandemonium broke loose in the courtroom, with reporters racing for the front seats. Bill Shelton, following Phil's instructions, began the direct questioning scathingly, seeming to be more prosecutor than defense attorney. Mr. A's patients at first were shocked, but by proceeding this way Shelton managed to bring out the names of many well-known business

116

and professional people whom Phil had effectively treated.

Then the prosecutor took over, and as Phil waited for Ken Masters' first barrage of questions, he thought, "I like this man. There's mutual respect here. But he's out to get me, and I'm not going to let him do it if I can help it." So the game was on, and all day long Masters plied him with repetitious questions, hoping to trip him up in one of his answers, or wear him down.

"I was receiving constant inner instructions from The Ring," Phil says of the trial. "I was not only receiving the answers, but also his questions in advance, so that I frequently found myself responding before he could finish framing his question. This visibly annoyed him, but the Powers were certainly with me that day. In midafternoon I looked over at Tim O'Grady. He had beads of perspiration over his upper lip and was like an animal ready to spring. I caught his eye and smiled, amused at his seriousness, and his whole expression changed. He too relaxed. Finally the prosecutor sprang at me, pointing his finger, and demanded, 'Why do you put your ear on their chests?'

" 'To listen to the vibrations,' I replied. 'Did you ever hear them?' "

" 'Oh, hell!' he exploded. Then, whirling around, he again pointed his finger at me and shouted, 'By listening to these so-called vibrations, you determine this and you determine that?' gesturing to various parts of the body, and I replied, 'Who can determine what? I touch a toe, and a headache leaves. Sometimes I touch a head and a toe ache leaves. Who knows about nerves?' "

Shaking his head, the prosecutor remarked to a woman who was crossing the courtroom, "Lady, will you have my chair? You can do as well as I'm doing." Shortly thereafter the prosecutor signaled the judge that he was finished, and Mr. A stepped down. The trial continued with a few more witnesses, before each attorney addressed the jury in closing arguments.

The jury was out for only twenty minutes. The unanimous verdict was "acquittal," and newspapers reported the outcome in front-page banner headlines. The following afternoon, when Phil arrived from San Francisco to resume his practice in Vallejo, the area around Mrs. Reed's house where he treated patients was so jammed with new ones that Mr. A could not make a passage through. He kept telling them his name, asking them to let him get inside, but they were not about to give up their place in line, so several retorted, "Yeah? Tell it to Sweeney." Mr. A got in his car and drove back to San Francisco.

Again, as in Reno many years earlier, he was the "Miracle Man" who went unrecognized.

CHAPTER VIII

# Public Demonstrations

After the trial Mr. A continued working six days a week alternating between San Francisco and Vallejo, without further interference. His wife, Rae, had wanted to attend the court trial, but he had forbidden it. She was supremely happy with the outcome, though, and with the glowing reports she received about her husband's testimony, and was eager to tell her family in Salt Lake City all about it. Toward the end of March, 1945, she told Phil that she planned to visit her relatives the first of April. He suggested that she delay a week in order for him to make arrangements with his patients that would enable him to join her, but she said she wanted to be there for her father's birthday and "to plan a surprise."

"But what if you get one of your attacks, and I'm not there to help you?" Phil cautioned.

"I'll be all right," she insisted.

Since she was clearly determined to go, Mr. A reserved a drawing room on the train for her and promised to follow the next week. The day after her arrival in Salt Lake City, a telegram from her sister informed him that Rae had died that morning in the hospital, of a heart attack.

Phil tried desperately to get reservations on a plane or train, but the war was still on, and none was available. He therefore set off cross-country in his 1939 Hudson car equipped with a fifty-gallon butane tank, so that if he lacked sufficient gas coupons he could run on that. He left town just as the train for Salt Lake City pulled out of the station, and driving without stopping, he arrived several hours ahead of it. He spent the evening with Rae's family, and then, because he couldn't get a room at Hotel Utah, he sat up all night in the lobby.

After the funeral the director of the mortuary, who knew of Mr. A's work, urged him to give a demonstration before returning to San Francisco, but Phil was not in the mood. He and Rae's sister began sorting her belongings, and while doing so found notes outlining why she had wanted to precede Phil to Salt Lake City. Her brother-in-law the doctor had been trying to convince her family that Mr. A was a quack, and she had wanted to display the reams of testimonials and newpaper reports of the trial while Phil was not around. Phil was so touched by her loyalty that he agreed to hold a demonstration for her relatives. The mortician, delighted, showed him a newspaper clipping in that day's edition, which carried a picture of a woman with Parkinson's disease and a plea for assistance from any doctor or method that could help her, since she was unable to lift her arms to feed herself or comb her hair.

"Let's go," Phil said, and the two set off to the woman's house. Within minutes after generating the energy, Phil watched the woman excitedly stretching her arms above her head, combing her hair, and holding a cup of coffee to her lips, but he cautioned that this seemingly marvelous effect was only temporary. "It would be necessary for the energy to rebuild your magnetic field with a series of treatments," he told her, "before the improvement will hold."

The mortician set the demonstration for two days later, and it was Phil's impression that only Rae's immediate family was to attend, but when he arrived at the mortuary the huge parking area was jammed. "This many relatives?" he exclaimed, but the mortician merely grinned.

Phil was frankly embarrassed at the thought of working before a large group of strangers, but he rolled up his sleeves and began on the volunteer patients, one by one. The first was a famous wrestler who had become so crippled that two men had to help him out of his car. Phil generated the energy through him, and within minutes the wrestler went into his act, swinging his legs, feinting, punching the air, and rough-housing with Mr. A. The audience, familiar with the wrestler's previous condition, sat stunned and then began to cheer. Others from the audience were equally benefited, and when the demonstration ended people swarmed around Mr. A, pleading for his autograph. Some even went down on their knees before him until he indignantly declared he would have none of that! It was the Power working through him, he said. He was merely the instrument.

Phil was unaware that any reporters had been present, until a next day's headline in *The Deseret News* announced: MIRACLE MAN GIVES DERN LIFT. The lengthy article read in part: "Old Ira (The Turk) Dern rides again—I mean runs! The maestro of wrestling in this skyline country actually ran and jumped yesterday for the first time in three years, as a crowd of friends and admirers looked on, pop-eyed. Dern, as most sports followers know, has been *hors de combat* with a dread crippling disease for more than three years. 'Li'l Arthur' as he calls the stuff in his system, has had him flat on his back at times. Now Turk Dern rides again. He showed me how it all happened, but nobody except an eyewitness would believe it. I don't even believe it yet, and I was there.

"Dern took me down to the Deseret Mortuary where I figured he would pick himself out a nice, cozy box, but instead he drove around to the annex where Manager Chick Merrill was waiting with a husky, handsome, gray-haired gentleman whom he introduced as [real name of Mr. A]. Chick had gathered together quite a few of the sick and the afflicted to whom he announced that [Mr. A] could help them get back their health. The "Miracle Man' took off his coat, rolled up his sleeves and went to work. He put holds on Dern the big boy never heard of in wrestling. He manipulated all of his joints and pressed the nerve centers mightily, and soon had Ira scratching the back of his neck, bending his knees and hoisting his arms, stunts he hadn't been able to do for two years.

"After about thirty minutes of this, Dern went out and walked up the steep steps of the mortuary, one step ahead of the other instead of the half step lift he had been doing for so long. Then he ran ten yards three different times and did a standing broad jump of about three feet. He was as tickled as a tot that had just taken its first steps." The article went on to describe other seeming miracles performed on people at the demonstration. Afterward a group of local businessmen offered to establish a large building where Phil could work, at a tempting fee, but he responded, "No, this work cannot be corralled." His inner instructions were guiding him back to California.

Before Phil left, the sports editor of *The Deseret News* brought a well-known medical doctor who asked him to work on a patient of his whose blood pressure was dangerously high and could not be lowered. While the physician continuously checked the patient's pressure with his pressure gauge, the energy Phil was generating dropped it a point a minute for eleven minutes. The excited doctor then asked Phil if he would accompany him to see several other of his most difficult cases. They set out together, and the first patient was a woman on whose knee the doctor had operated. Since then she had been unable to bend it, but after Mr. A buzzed it with energy, the knee moved easily.

"I was puzzled by the woman," he recalls, "because instead of seeming happy with the results, she appeared troubled instead. But when the doctor and I went outside, he explained that the woman had filed a malpractice suit against him."

They called on several other patients, including a bedridden boy in critical condition with rheumatic fever, and when the doctor checked him after Phil's treatment, he kept saying, "Amazing, amazing! There is great improvement here."

To Mr. A's chagrin, the sports editor who had accompanied them on the rounds printed a full account in the newspaper the following morning, and Phil decided it was time to head for San Francisco and a little more privacy. He resumed his interrupted practice, but now people began making the trek from the Salt Lake area to receive his ministrations.

Franklin Delano Roosevelt died on April 12, 1945, and our war-weary nation had a new President, Harry S Truman. Victory in Europe came May 6, and in mid-August Japan surrendered. Peace had returned at last. Immediately afterward Mr. A made plans for a trip to St. Paul to visit his brother and sister, whom he had not seen in many years, but while generating energy to a patient in his Bay Area office he received from The Ring a different kind of instruction. As clearly as if it had been spoken aloud, the information came, "You are to marry a girl in Salt Lake City whom you have not yet met. Stop off there. You will know her when you see her."

Always attentive in his inner instructions, Phil stopped overnight in Salt Lake City enroute to Minnesota, and although he saw several attractive girls in and out of the lobby, he knew that none was the one. Then he walked into the hotel's coffee shop and saw her. The inner knowing was immediately responsive, but he gave her no sign. The next morning a bellboy whom Phil had treated on a previous visit was helping him with his luggage, and Mr. A asked, "Who is the tall girl in the coffee shop?"

Mentioning her name, he said, "She's the manager."

"Well," Phil replied with a smile, "I'm going to marry her, but she doesn't know it. I'm on my way to Minnesota, but I'll stop off here again on my way home."

Gasoline was still being rationed, and Mr. A was

traveling by rail. At the depot in Omaha where he changed trains, a girl rushed up and threw her arms around him, saying, "Oh, Doctor, I'm so glad to see you again." Embarrassed, Phil said nothing until she added, "Don't you remember touching my face at that demonstration in Salt Lake City? I was the one with Bell's palsy, and I have never had a trace of it since!"

After a week's visit with his brother and sister, Phil arrived back in Salt Lake City, and this time he was introduced to tall, good-looking Bea. They found that they enjoyed each other's company, and since she was shortly to have a vacation, he suggested she spend it in California. For a week or so she visited friends in the Bay Area. Then she wanted to see her sister in Los Angeles, and Phil drove her there. While in Los Angeles he telephoned his old friend Manly P. Hall, author of the scholarly and enormously successful *An Encyclopedic Outline of Masonic, Hermetic, Quabbalistic and Rosicrucian Symbolical Philosophy*, an interpretation of the secret teachings concealed within the rituals and mysteries of all ages.

Hall had for some time been urging his overworked friend to take time off to visit Los Angeles and inspect the operation of his Philosophical Research Society, and now he took him on a tour, exhibiting the various collections and introducing him to the staff. Then he suggested that Mr. A give a demonstration of his healing work the next day, and he did so, with his usual success.

Bea returned to Salt Lake City after her vacation, but their wedding date was set for the following February, on St. Valentine's Day. Phil could not return to Salt Lake City without articles about him appearing in the newspapers, so he went to Ogden for the marriage license a few days beforehand. Again an enterprising reporter found out about it, and articles appeared with flamboyant headlines like: FAMOUS MIRACLE MAN TAKES BRIDE. A photograph of Mr. A rather than the bride accompanied the accounts, and Bea wondered what she was getting into.

Following the wedding, Bea's mother accompanied them to her hometown in Utah, where Phil could meet her brother and sisters. That evening, when the brother complained of shortness of breath and chronic neck and shoulder pains, Mr. A treated him, and the symptoms disappeared. The next morning the new bridegroom, discovering he had left his razor in Salt Lake City, went to the barbershop for a shave, but the town barber dolefully remarked, "I can cut your hair, but I can't shave you because I have such bad arthritis in my fingers."

"If your fingers can be fixed so that you can shave me, will you do it?" Phil asked, and the puzzled barber agreed. Mr. A buzzed the energy through the barber's fingers, and then received a perfect shave. But news travels fast in a small town, and before Phil could leave the barbershop, strangers were lining up for his help.

Bea's nephew, a boy in knee pants, told his new uncle, "I never feel good." His mother explained that the boy suffered from an advanced heart condition with hypertension, resulting from rheumatic fever, and when Mr. A generated the energy through him, he exclaimed, "Gee, that weight is off my chest. I feel good clear to my toes." Some years later he was in ROTC, and hoping for a commission, but because of his early medical record there was a question about his heart. He went to the Bay Area to receive more energizing from his uncle and was soon commissioned. Now he is a major in the Air Force, and has been stationed in many distant places throughout the world.

After visiting with her relatives, Bea and Phil continued their honeymoon through the national parks, before returning to his practice in the Bay Area. During the Christmas holidays they brought from Lake Tahoe a nine-foot silver-tip tree, and Bea decorated it with the usual bangles and newtype bubble lights. Friends came in to see her handiwork, and she was proudly snapping a picture of it when Mr. A, to tease her, sent a blast of energy through his fingers toward the tree across the room. The picture caught what closely resembles forked lightning.

During the next Christmas season Phil and Bea went to Los Angeles to visit her sister, whose husband owned racehorses. Many of them were ailing, and the Santa Anita track was about to open. Phil's brother-in-law urged him to try his remarkable energies on the horses, and although he protested that he knew nothing about them, he accompanied him to the stables at Santa Anita. Brother-in-law Jack introduced Mr. A to the trainer, and when he mentioned Phil's mysterious power the trainer mumbled, "To hell with the horses. I've got troubles of my own. I'm just out of bed with pneumonia. How about helping me?"

Fascinated by the new energy which Phil gave him, he said, "I've got two barns full of horses and most of 'em are sick. The veterinarian is doing what he can for 'em, and I'm trying to get 'em ready for the races, but it's pretty discouraging. Some have kidney trouble, and you name it . . . they've got it."

In the barns, Phil listened to the vibrations from their chests and decided they were no different from the tone system of a human being. He therefore began treating the racers, and as they received the energy they would affectionately reach around to pull his hair and nip at his shirt. While Mr. A was sitting beneath Sun Cap, with the stallion's hind legs in front of him, the trainer became concerned, saying, "Listen, Phil, he's liable to kick the daylights out of you." But whenever Sun Cap would jerk a leg during the treatment, he would hold it steady until Phil guided it down to the ground.

Watching the astonishing display of affection, the trainer harrumphed, "Well, you wouldn't get me in that position under that stallion." Whenever Phil stood in front of Sun Cap, the horse would gently nip at his shirt as if to detain him, and the trainer said, "The truth of the matter is, this horse is in love with you. In fact, so are the others that you treated."

Since Mr. A's offices in San Francisco were being moved to a new location and were not yet ready to receive clients, Phil took a more extended vacation than usual. The racing season began, and one day the trainer stopped Phil to say, "I've got two barns full of well horses, and the damn fools are on a picnic. I can't do anything with them. They run when they want to, and they don't when they don't want to. They just don't care for nothing."

The day before Sun Cap was to run, Mr. A gave him another energy treatment. Sun Cap was known as a fast horse, but his legs had been fired and he had not won a race for some time. The next day Sun Cap would be pitted against a "favorite" who had been winning every race, at whatever distance. Mr. A, to whom racing was a novelty, bet forty-five dollars on Sun Cap across the board and the race was on, with the favored horse taking a long lead and Sun Cap loping along at the rear of the pack for half the distance. The he took off, catching up with the lead horse, but in the homestretch the favorite again took the lead, with Sun Cap second. Then, just before the finish line Sun Cap leaped ahead, winning the race.

Jack and the trainer were jubilant, and Phil then learned that the latter had bet two thousand dollars on Sun Cap to win, after observing the results of the treatments. They wanted Mr. A to stay and work on Sun Cap some more, so he could be entered in "the big race," which covered a longer distance than the horse had ever raced, but Phil returned to his human patients in San Francisco.

# CHAPTER IX

## The Middle Years

Phil had barely settled into his new office when a woman came in, writing with pain and crying that "my whole body is burning up inside." Pleadingly, she added, "I have exhausted every other medical source, but I've heard what you can do. Please help me!"

Mr. A put his ear to her chest, then generated the energy, and the next day she came back for more, ecstatically describing how much better she felt. The following day her attorney arrived, saying, "I understand that you helped a client of mine—Mrs. Leo. I wonder if you can help me. My pelvis was crushed in a bicycle accident as a boy, and I've been in pain ever since."

Phil sensed that the lawyer had come merely out of curiosity, but he accommodated him, and to the lawyer's surprise his pain disappeared. During and after the treatment he regaled Mr. A with stories of his own importance, saying that he was chief counsel for one of the big railroads and that whenever he came to the office he must be treated immediately. "My time is terribly important," he puffed, "and I don't have time to wait for Christ Himself."

Sizing up his new patient, Mr. A replied, "Well, mister, as far as I'm concerned you're simply another

X in my book and must wait your turn like all the others."

The lawyer glared, turned on his heel, and left, slamming the door so violently that Phil expected the glass to shatter. A few days later Mrs. Leo returned, giggling with glee and saying, "I understand my friend Broder was here. He's absolutely furious with you! He's not accustomed to it, but I'm so happy that you put him in his place. We've known each other since childhood, and he's a brilliant attorney, but we've been fighting all our lives."

Phil told Mrs. Leo, as he had the lawyer, that the man's pain would return until his magnetic field was fully charged, but he never came back. During Mrs. Leo's occasional visits for further treatment, she would report on Attorney Broder, saying, "I go to his office now and then about my legal affairs, and when he groans and complains about his pain, I say to him, 'If you really want help, I know a man who. . . .' Then I leave quickly, while he rages about your refusal to take him ahead of other patients. He keeps going to doctors, but he's getting no better."

Many years later Mrs. Leo told Mr. A that Broder was dying. "He's been bleeding internally and has been in the hospital receiving numerous blood transfusions. When the doctors told him they could do nothing more for him, he insisted on going home to die. I still quarrel with him, but I don't want him to die."

"What are you trying to tell me?" Phil asked gently. "That you want me to try to help him?"

"Oh, I wish you would," she said eagerly.

"All right, call him and tell him I'll come to his

home to give him one charge of energy. But if it helps him enough to get out of bed he must come to my office if he wants further treatments and wait his turn. Make sure he agrees to this before I'll go." Mrs. Leo joyously made the telephone call, and Broder accepted the terms.

Broder's apartment had a large picture window overlooking the Golden Gate, and from his deathbed he could watch the ships plying in and out of the harbor. When Phil greeted him, the attorney said gruffly, "What do you think you're going to do for me? The best doctors in the West have informed me there's nothing more to be done, and I'm so weak now I can't get out of this bed."

"'Sounds like you're in a bad way," Mr. A sympathized, as he prepared to listen to his chest vibrations. Then he sent the energy charging through the frail body, and in twenty minutes the attorney was out of bed and stalking around the room.

After watching his antics for a few minutes, Mr. A said, "Now you'd better call my wife and explain why I'm late getting home for dinner." The attorney quickly dialed the number Phil gave him, and when Bea answered he said, "That husband of yours is here and he put me back on my feet. I understand that you're from Utah. I want you to know that I'm also a Mormon on Sunday, because I listen to the Tabernacle choir on radio. I'm a Catholic on Friday because my wife feeds me fish, and I'm a Mason the rest of the time." Clearly, he was feeling frisky. As Mr. A waved good-bye to him from the door, Broder began, "Now, when you come tomorrow. . . ."

Wheeling, Phil said, "What did you say?"

"Oh, I'll be in your office tomorrow," Broder replied quickly.

The lawyer was there when Mr. A arrived and continued to adorn the outer office at regular intervals, waiting his turn. But his disposition did not match his physical improvement. Once as he dropped his coat on the sofa it slid onto the floor, and he staged a tantrum. Phil listened to his chest and, noting that the vibrations were calm, said, "You're an actor! You weren't in a temper, and there is no inner emotion."

"Why, you so-and-so"—Broder grinned—"you're the only one who ever nailed me on that one. I'm glad a jury doesn't know."

They became good friends, and once, like Attorney Tim O'Grady several years earlier, Broder said, "I wish you'd get in trouble, because for appreciation and affection I want to show you how good I am." Uneasily, Mr. A wondered if this might portend more trouble ahead, but he listened inwardly and received no flash of anything but smooth sailing. Broder eventually retired from active law practice, and in 1957 Mr. A read in the newspaper that the attorney had dropped dead of a heart seizure.

Phil telephoned Broder's wife and learned that anger —this time genuine—had been his friend's undoing when he received word that a panel of judges had rejected his application for a full pardon for one of his former clients whom he still believed to be innocent. Anger and fear—the body's greatest enemies!

One evening Mr. A was invited by a friend to go to a dinner honoring the Governor of California, and before the speeches began Phil was taken to the head table for an introduction, whereupon the governor said, "I was about to call for you over the loudspeaker, because I'd heard you were here. See this tumor on my finger? The doctor wants to operate on it, but can you fix it?"

Embarrassed, Phil replied, "This is an awkward place to work with you."

"Then will you come to the reception afterward?" the governor pressed. At the reception, standing off in a corner, Phil generated the energy to his finger, and the lump disappeared before their eyes. The governor was so delighted that he said, "Here is my unlisted telephone number. Whenever you're going through Sacramento, I want you to come to the mansion and see us."

Three days later the governor telephoned to say he was on his way back to Sacramento and would like to drop by Phil's house. Bea, in typical feminine fashion, began exclaiming that her hair was a mess and she couldn't possibly receive the governor looking like that, so Mr. A turned back to the telephone, saying, "Governor, it's like this. My wife says you can't come now, but I'll be going through Sacramento in a day or two, and I'll see you there."

The two men became close friends, and whenever the governor saw Bea he would tease her about turning away a governor from her door. He used to stop in frequently to visit the A's, and they would repay his visits when they drove through Sacramento enroute to Lake Tahoe.

The second time they dined at the governor's mansion, a woman psychic was present who claimed to be able to foresee coming events. She tried to draw Phil into making predictions, but he laughingly said that was not his field. The governor had been detained, and the First Lady of California finally sighed, "I wonder how long it will be before he comes home. He's at the legislature, and they're debating a water project—it will probably go on all night."

Without thinking, Phil blurted, "At eleven o'clock he will call to say that the legislature is deadlocked and he's on his way home." Mrs. Marsh, the psychic who had fruitlessly tried to interest Mr. A in predictions, gasped, "You made a direct statement! You'd better be right!"

It was growing late, and after dinner the A's wanted to leave, but the governor's wife insisted on taking them on a tour of the mansion. Then the telephone rang, and looking at her watch, she exclaimed, "It's eleven o'clock." She took down the receiver and heard her husband say that since the legislature was now hopelessly deadlocked for the night, he was on his way home. Then she excitedly told him that nearly three hours earlier, Mr. A had told her this would happen at the exact time.

On another occasion at the mansion, the governor grilled Phil like a cross-examiner, saying, "I want to find out what makes you tick. I've never met anyone like you!" He was on his way to a conference in Hawaii, and immediately on returning he telephoned Phil, saying, "I've got real trouble in my neck. I had an adjustment in Hawaii, and I've been in constant pain ever since. Can I come over?"

"Come ahead," Phil said, and after his pain was released the governor inscribed his special first-day cover of the convention program to Mr. A, saying, "Only fifty were issued, one for each governor, and I want you to have mine for your collection."

The next morning, while Mr. A was generating more energy to him, the governor said, "There's something I would like very much to read, and that is the transcript of your medical trial at Vallejo. I've heard it was quite a trial, and I'm curious, especially since Ken Masters was prosecuting. I know that man, and he's good!" Phil dug out the transcript, and the governor spent several hours reading it, from time to time saying excitedly to his wife, "Listen to this!" He would then read her excerpts from the testimony.

During this period, a salesman who was handling the disposal of lots for Phil at Lake Tahoe telephoned to say that a dental technician had selected two lots for purchase, and could Mr. A go to her house in San Jose to complete the deal? As soon as Phil could get away from the office he drove over, but she greeted him at the door. "You'll have to come back another time. I've been sitting in front of the fireplace all morning trying to get relief from terribly painful lumbago, and I'm simply not up to talking business today."

Phil, who had driven all the way down from the East Bay Area, said he wouldn't have time to come back. "But if lumbago is all that's bothering you, we can take care of that in a few minutes." Unaware of Phil's identity, she expressed her doubts. But after he had sent the energy through her, she kept exclaiming, "I can't find it. It's gone! What did you do?"

Grinning, Mr. A said, "I'm sorry. I forgot to tell you that although I came here to close the sale on two lots, working with energy is my regular occupation."

137

She continued to look puzzled but readily signed the deal for the property.

Phil also treated his in-laws. Bea's cousin had a severe heart condition, and her teen-age daughter had a collapsed lung and excessive scar tissue resulting from the removal of a ruptured appendix when she was two years old. Following his energy treatments their conditions cleared up, and a quarter of a century later both mother and daughter are still enjoying excellent health.

Marie, another of Bea's relatives, came from Arizona for energy treatments, complaining of migraine headaches, which quickly disappeared. The next summer she came again to visit, at a time when California was reporting a number of polio cases, and another cousin frantically telephoned Mr. A to come immediately, saying, "Something is terribly wrong with Marie.".

Phil says of the case, "They had her laid out on the bed, but her body was jerking out of control. Her head was pulled back, her pelvis was jerking, and her feet and legs were tense in spasm. Listening to her vibrations, I realized that the pressure of the legs had to be relieved immediately to take the strain off the body and heart. To do this, the energy was generated to the nerve centers in the bottom of each foot. Then the energy adjusted the magnetic field and condensing system, which had been jolted out of control. In a matter of minutes the jerking ceased, and she relaxed. Within fifteen minutes she was up and going. I remember having been brought into a similar case when I was just a boy. Then they referred to it as spinal meningitis."

Another of Mr. A's patients was a registered nurse

in San Francisco, whose rapid heartbeat he slowed to normal through the energy treatments; but later, imagining that she had adhesions and other ills resulting from an earlier operation, she persuaded a surgeon to perform an exploratory operation. While she was still hospitalized, the doctor called Phil, saying, "See if you can handle this character. I can't! Anyway, she insists on seeing you, but she's in a two-bed room, and the other woman is not my patient."

Mr. A obligingly dropped by the hospital to see the woman, and she began bouncing around the bed, describing her woes so comically that the other patient in the room said. "I can't keep from laughing at you two, and it's killing me. I've just had rectal surgery and I'm in agony." She then began moaning, but Mr. A dared not treat her. Feeling sorry for her, however, he removed the platinum ring from his finger and charged it with her matching energy. Then he told her to hold it in the palm of her hand, and she immediately exclaimed, "The pain's gone! What happened?"

A friend of Bea's who had been an outstanding dress designer in Utah, until ill health forced her retirement, came to San Francisco to see Mr. A. She was in the habit of losing consciousness frequently from heart seizures, and her body was badly swollen; but when the bloating and heart attacks miraculously disappeared after Phil's treatments, she refused to leave the Bay Area where his services were readily at hand. She went to work in an executive capacity at one of the leading stores, and while coming in regularly for treatments to rebuild her magnetic field, she discovered that the lowgrade tissue energy, and the sores which used to break out on her body, no longer troubled her.

Mrs. Nell Hickman, a member of Manly Hall's Philosophical Research Society in Los Angeles, sent Olive Stuart, an opera singer, to Phil for treatment, and she was so happy with her improved health and breathing that she continued to make the trek to San Francisco at regular intervals.

In 1957 Mrs. Stuart asked Mr. A to see a boy with polio, who had been living between an iron lung and a rocking-bed for three years. The boy's father also sent a pleading letter, and when Mr. A arrived at their house in Phoenix the boy was lying on a rocking-bed. Phil sent the energy through his abdominal area, and he began breathing deeply. His parents explained that the doctors had told the lad to breathe against a sand-bag to test the strength of his abdominal muscles, but that all he could manage was a quarter-pound one. Pushing one of his fists into the boy's belly, Phil said, "Take a deep breath. Now push my fist out with your muscles." He did, and the parents sighed with relief. The boy then began breathing normally, the iron lung and rocking-bed were soon discarded, and he began going to football games and dances.

Mrs. Stuart had arranged for Mr. A to give a demonstration of his work while in Phoenix, but that afternoon she came to him saying agitatedly that she had just learned that a group of local doctors was planning to attend. "Will this interfere with you?" she asked.

"No," Phil said, and added with a chuckle, "It may be interesting."

That evening Phil watched from a seat in the auditorium as the audience began to assemble. There was a cross section of cripples and sick people, many of whom had to be assisted to their seats. Then four doctors and a nurse arrived, and Mr. A went to the platform, saying to the audience, "I want you to understand that this demonstration is for the purpose of showing the speed of the energy and the effect that it has on ailments. The results may not be lasting, until the energy field is built up to secure it. Now, who wants to be first?"

A woman in the front row came up to take the chair that had been placed in front of him, and Phil asked, "Is there a doctor or nurse in the house who would like to check these cases before and after?".

The nurse beat the others to the platform, but when she requested a stethoscope, a doctor in the audience retrieved one from his car outside and then took over the checking. One after another, he agreed that the first twelve cases had registered prompt improvement. Then a woman in the audience stood up and began questioning the doctor on his credentials, believing him to be "a part of the act." The local physician, who had never seen Mr. A, indignantly recited his medical degrees and experience, then left the stage to rejoin his colleagues, exclaiming, "I know what I've been listening to, and what I heard." At the end of the demonstration the doctor came up to congratulate Mr. A, saying, "It has been an enjoyable and fascinating evening. I am amazed with the speed of the energy and the results obtained on this variety of ailments. Whenever you're in the area again, I hope you will come to see me."

# CHAPTER X

## Not in the Textbooks

For many years Mr. A had known, through his inner instructions, that one day he would meet a person who would seek to understand his work with the energies, and who would "have what it takes" to acquire the necessary qualifications to handle its application. Not until 1956, however, did Mr. A receive word from "The Ring" that the time was now right for him to give a demonstration of the energies in Los Angeles, so that he could meet the person with whom he was to deal. Since friends had long been urging him to come there, he notified them that they could arrange for a demonstration, and two days later the date was set.

At this session in Los Angeles, the first person to come forward was an overweight but nice-looking girl in her late teens, who said that since birth she had suffered from the kind of ailment which is sometimes referred to as "canary heart." Phil asked why she thought that the energy would help her, and she uttered the code which was his confirmation that this was the long-awaited person. She also informed him that she was going to be a doctor.

Sensing her vibrations as he leaned his ear to her chest, Phil murmured silently, "Oh, oh, here she is."

Outwardly, though, he gave no sign, and after sending the energy to her magnetic field, he then continued the demonstration by treating the others who were there for help. His friend Manly P. Hall was among those present, and afterward he and the others urged Mr. A to come regularly to Los Angeles. Since his inner instructions had already told him to do so, he agreed to come once or twice a month.

"After that," he recently told me, "whenever I was in Los Angeles this youngster would be there, saying she 'had to have the energy' and that she 'had to be a doctor.' For six months I barely acknowledged her presence, except to send the energy through her, and some of the others complained I was indifferent to her. Actually, I was testing her. I wanted to be sure she was qualified. At that time she was in premed, and whenever I was in Los Angeles working she would come early before her classes, and after classes she would be back again, driving fifty miles each way from her college in Pomona. I kept needling her, asking why she needed all that energy, and she would invariably reply, 'I've got to have it. I've got to understand it, and I've got to be a doctor.' That is all she would say."

The girl was Dena L. Smith, who is now an accomplished doctor and surgeon, living in California. Because of her continuing interest, she has thoroughly investigated Mr. A's work and is convinced that the world needs to know more about this Ancient Wisdom of healing which flows so freely through his fingers. While preparing the material for this book, I talked at length with Dr. Smith and asked that she describe her introduction to Mr. A. This is what she told me: "I had never felt well, and my heartbeat was very irregular. But I was determined to be a doctor, and because I desperately needed energy I was eating so much that I was overweight. In 1955 one of my college friends told me about a man in San Francisco who gave energy through the laying on of hands. I was then in premed at Pomona College in California, and I said to her, 'If this man is ever where I can get to him, will you let me know?' I felt I had to meet him.

"A year passed, and one day the same friend told me that Mr. A was going to give a demonstration at the home of Marta Burleigh in Los Angeles. I said I wanted to go, no matter what I might miss in classes that day, and we went. When I saw him come into the room, I felt I had known him forever, and when the demonstration started, I was the first to reach him. He listened to my chest and then, without comment, began sending the energy through my lower abdomen. Within minutes my heartbeat became regular and has remained so ever since.

"But I knew that I still needed energy, and that I had to learn more about this remarkable process. From that point on, whenever Mr. A came to Los Angeles, I would get up at dawn to drive into town before classes, and again that evening—two hundred miles a day. He would ask why I kept coming, and he never encouraged me, but I didn't give a thought to the drive or the time involved. It just seemed the most important thing for me to do. When he saw I was determined to learn more about this method of helping people, he gradually began to let me in on some of the cases by allowing me to listen to their hearts. He would explain what the tone variations meant to him, and then let me hear the rapid changes made by the energy."

Dena says she will never forget the first case: "a woman who complained of double vision since striking her head in a fall from a swing over an Arizona canyon."

"The woman said she had been to many doctors and specialists," Dena recalls, "but there had been no improvement. Mr. A listened to her chest, and then while I listened to it he explained what I was hearing. As he began sending the energy through the woman's lower abdomen, she complained that it was her eyes, not her belly that was bothering her, but he continued to feed her eyes through the pelvic area, and then balanced the energy at the base of her skull. He told her first to cover one eye, then the other, and when she was permitted to uncover both at once, she exclaimed, 'Oh, they are together! It's not double anymore.' Then she asked if she should come again, and Mr. A replied, 'Why come if your vision is normal?' She never needed another session, and you can imagine how impressed and excited I was."

By this time Dena's own health was superb, and her extra weight had melted away. When it was time for her to apply for admission to medical school she faced a real handicap, however, because at that time it was difficult for a woman to gain admission. Most of her classmates, even those of highest scholastic standing, were playing it safe and applying to a number of colleges, but Mr. A told Dena, "Apply only to the University of Southern California School of Medicine." She did so, and was accepted.

During her four years in medical school, and her subsequent year of internship at Los Angeles County General Hospital, Mr. A came every second weekend to Los Angeles for a three-day working session. On those Saturday afternoons Dena would review with him what she had learned during the interval and would ply him with questions.

"It was uncanny," she recalls. "No matter what disease or ailment I had studied and observed during the previous two weeks, invariably a person suffering from that identical condition would be the first patient in on Sunday morning to see Mr. A, and I was there to check on what the energies could do. For instance, during one such period we had been studying tuberculosis in the hospital wards, and when Mr. A came to Los Angeles I asked him, 'Do I have to be worried about getting TB? Most of those we observe are virulent cases, and the other students are taking prophylactic drugs as a preventative.' Mr. A replied, 'No, you're full of the bug. It's always there, in anyone. You don't have to worry as long as your energy is up. The germs can't eat healthy tissue, only dormant tissue. It's the same with those who are working with lepers. Some contract it and others don't, depending on the strength of their energy fields.'

"Doctors used to treat some cases of TB by collapsing a lung, and we had been studying those cases that week," Dena continued. "The first person who came to Mr. A Sunday morning was such a case. I listened, and his heart was irregular and labored. His left lung was full of rales and noisy wheezes, but I could hear nothing in the right one, so I exclaimed, 'This lung is collapsed.' Mr. A worked on the left lung first, then told me to listen to the right one. Suddenly there was a hollow slaplike sound, and I immediately could hear breath sounds. I realized that the energy had reexpanded the right lung, but I couldn't believe what I was hearing, because in medical school we are taught that once a lung is collapsed, that's it. It scars down permanently, the books say. I asked Mr. A how he could have effected such a seeming miracle, and he replied matter-of-factly, 'That's how the energy works.' Elaborating further on tuberculosis, he said, 'The energy revitalizes the good lung tissue so that it has the strength to slough off the infected tissue. It simply sets the charge for the good tissue to resist infection.' He made it sound simple, but I was baffled."

After studying about polio, Dena proudly took her new knowledge to Mr. A, wondering what his explanation of this would be. "In my opinion," he replied, "as it is explained to me over the air it is simply the result of atmospheric life energy storms. Have you noticed how the so-called epidemics usually occur during the summer when lightning storms are common in different parts of the country? This sets up a turbulence in the human energy patterns which I call energy storms, and when the human condensing system is not strong enough to protect the magnetic field from the jolt of the distorted energy, the field then goes into spasm. There is more likelihood of being hit in the water, because one is grounded. This can happen even in a bathtub. Also, atmospheric human wave storms can disturb the human energy patterns, resulting in backaches and other minor physical problems, when the body's energy is only moderately depleted and not completely optimal."

Dena says she constantly argued with Mr. A in those years, refusing to accept his explanations until she had actually seen the force at work and checked out the results in each case. Nothing like this was included in her medical textbooks. As an example, when she asked him about mononucleosis, the so-called kissing disease of young people, which is thought to be infectious, Mr. A declared that it is a condition resulting from emotional repression and sexual starvation at this time in life.

She wanted to know about multiple sclerosis and related neurologic diseases, and Mr. A replied, "As it comes over the air to me, these ailments are caused from prolonged seething and jealousy." Astonished, Dena began checking into the personal history of such cases which came to her attention, and she recently told me that in every instance she has found corroboration for his statement.

Continuing to recall other experiences, Dena said, "Often over the years, when Mr. A would tell me to place my fingers on a glaucoma patient's eyes as he generated the energy to what he calls the eye centers in the lower pelvis, I was repeatedly astounded when the eye pressure would release and the eyes would immediately soften under my fingers, while the patient expressed instant relief."

When she questioned Mr. A about his ideas on glaucoma, he replied, "It is easy for the energy to handle this condition, because lack of energy lets the eye liquid thicken so that the normal flow is impaired. In other words, the liquid calcium thickens and can't pass through the minute passages of the eye, and the pressure from this liquid builds up and does the damage.

When energy is generated to the master eye nerves in the magnetic field [the pelvic area], the eye softens because the liquid can flow normally out of the eye." Dena reports that when doctors have tested the pressure in their patients' eyeballs both before and after the sessions with Mr. A, they find that the pressure has dramatically dropped to normal. This affords only temporary relief, however, unless the energy is built up to retain the strength and eliminate the cause.

When Dena asked Mr. A about cataracts, he said, "As people get older and do less about keeping their energy up, they are more likely to develop cataracts. On the other hand, when they occur in infants it usually represents a blocked energy circuit to the eye nerves. Cataracts form from the lack of energy in the eye."

While Dena was learning about anemia in medical school, she asked Mr. A so many questions about it that he finally said, "I suppose you also think that the heart pumps blood throughout the entire body."

"Naturally," she responded.

"And I suppose you think that anemia results from a deficiency of red corpuscles in the blood?"

"Yes. How else?" She shrugged.

Grinning, Mr. A declared, "Well, I have news for you. My flashes say that the artery and vein fibers have one form of energy and the corpuscles have a different polarization. This interaction is what moves the blood and pushes the corpuscles in the arteries and veins. As soon as the energy is increased in the corpuscles this action is speeded up, pushing the blood over the head and eliminating the dizziness, etc. And by putting a charge of energy to the area of the relays to the heart, spleen, and pancreas, it seems immediately to increase the number and charge of the corpuscles [which Mr. A usually calls electrons].

"Incidentally, here is another one. Haven't you wondered why blood clots develop after surgery?"

Dena nodded, and Mr. A continued, "Well, the insult of the surgery to the nerves is a shock to the magnetic field, which in effect lowers the energy supply to the body, and this is often manifested in the formation of blood clots in the leg veins. It's simply that the energy of the vein nerve fibers and the charge of energy in the blood are not adequate to provide the necessary push power to the blood, and it slows down and clots. Back in the early 1930's we checked this out thoroughly in the hospital, and although early ambulation of patients will help by stimulating their adrenalin and vein walls through exercise, it is not the complete answer."

Flabbergasted by such seemingly revolutionary theories, Dena exclaimed, "Don't get mad at me! Don't get mad at me! I've got to figure this out. I've never heard anything like this before, and it's hard for me to comprehend it. In other words, what you say could explain why even early and immediate ambulation after surgery will not insure against developing these clots which are so deadly. But wait, if the heart doesn't pump the blood, as you say, then what does it do?"

"The heart simply recharges the electrons, the corpuscles," he replied. "When it doesn't have enough energy to recharge them, then anemia results from lack of the push power."

Recalling this astonishing discussion, Dena told me,

"The next day, as I watched Phil put a charge in the heart area of a woman with severe anemia, immediately her pale, pasty color became pink, and in a few moments she exclaimed, 'My feet are warm for the first time in years.' Warmth was permeating her entire body, and when she returned to her doctor for another hemoglobin count, it had dramatically returned to normal. She, like many other anemic patients, jubilantly brought in her before-and-after blood counts to prove the process."

I had the good fortune to sit in on a recent session with Mr. A and Dr. Smith while they were replaying their early discussions about various diseases. Dena, with the help of her carefully preserved notes, seemed to have total recall, and as I asked about certain ailments she could readily discuss them in terms of their much earlier conferences while she was in medical school.

"Arthritis seemed like such a baffling disease," Dena said. "Our textbooks conceded as much, but when I asked Mr. A about it, he told me, 'Arthritis results when the magnetic field does not pull enough energy from the lungs to supply the necessary energy to keep calcium liquid in the body. This is the way it comes over the air to me. If you break a bone, a shock is delivered to the field, which reverts back to the injured area, retarding the energy at that point and causing the calcium to solidify to mend the bone. This is nature's way of mending. But when the field has a general depletion of energy, the calcium solidifies in the weaker sections of the body, such as joints, etc.' "

Dena asked why children, then, can get arthritis,

and he replied, "Because the field was stunted at birth or thereafter, retarding its drawing power from the lungs, which can also bring about many other childhood ailments such as rheumatic fever, asthma, croup, colic, and hypertension which follows throughout life unless it is corrected with the energies."

Shortly after their first discussion of arthritis, Dena said, a sixteen-year-old girl hobbled into Phil's office with a look of great suffering. She had generalized arthritis and tender, swollen joints for which she had been unable to find relief from medical specialists. Dena recalls that the girl's body was unusually well developed for her years, and that after Mr. A brought her energy up to normal, she asked how she could prevent the arthritic condition from returning, without coming for periodic treatments to keep the charge built up. Explaining to her the cause of her difficulty, Mr. A suggested that when she could find a man born with certain frequencies complementary to her own astrological pattern, she should marry him to receive her needed fuel. A few years later she returned, glowing with health, to show off her two beautiful children. There was no sign of arthritis, and the young mother exclaimed, "You will never know how grateful I am to you. Several doctors had told me that I would be a cripple the rest of my life, but now I'm happily married and without pain."

During Dena's senior year at medical school, she and her classmates were delivering so many babies at the county hospital that it was necessary to work rapidly, almost in assembly-line fashion. She resented having to use forceps, and when she asked Mr. A about it he replied, "They'd be a lot better off to be born the natural way, as nature intended. Forceps can do irrevocable damage unless the shock can be released from the baby's magnetic field soon after birth. Also, if a mother is heavily sedated before giving birth, her own field is partially dormant and she imparts this shock to the infant. It is the same with spinal anesthesia, and it is the same when a mother in prolonged labor is so tense or afraid that this tension is automatically delivered to the field of the newborn, and there are many other facets. If this tension can be released from the field of the newborn, so it can draw its necessary capacity of energy from the lungs to the field, the infant is in harmony with the universe and will have a chance to grow and develop physically and mentally. The high priests of ancient days understood how to blend the energy to release these tensions and recharge the field. When the field was opened to the universe, by releasing any bondage delivered to it from the parent or from a forced or difficult birth, this was the Original Baptism, as it is explained to me over the air."

Dena asked why some babies are born with cerebral palsy and congenital heart defects, and he explained, "Most come from this tension of birth, which manifests itself in all the other ailments of childhood. Because such a baby lacks resistance, he is wide open to ailments, and this tension remains throughout life if it isn't released, subjecting such a person to a life plagued by ailments."

Dena says, "With my own ears I have heard the murmurs disappear from the heart of a child with a congenital heart defect who was scheduled to undergo open-heart surgery, so that the operation was later canceled, when the defect could not again be diagnosed."

People who have seen or heard the results of releasing the pressures and tensions after birth bring their newborn babies to Mr. A immediately after checking out of the hospital, so that the child will have a good start in life. Dena says that when Mr. A sends the proper energy through the infants' field, they immediately take a deep breath, stretch, yawn, and straighten their legs. Their color becomes normal, and they also develop a ravenous appetite.

I asked Mr. A for further enlightenment, and he said, "When a pregnant woman gets angry or tense, fearful or resentful, this tension is delivered to the baby's field. The mother should be relaxed and serene so that she will not tense her own field and give birth to a child who is angry and resentful."

During Dena's medical school training she once asked Mr. A, "What is cancer?"

His reply: "This is what has been explained to me over the air since my earliest memory. When the tissue doesn't receive the necessary life energy, then a weaker section of the tissue begins to deteriorate, shutting itself off from energy; the tissue dies and gas forms in the cells, causing bloat and expansion. Because of low energy, the live cells don't have the resistance to slough off the dead ones, so the dead cells deteriorate the live ones. It's something like one bad apple in a barrel gradually causing all the others to rot. When this condition exists, any shock or insult to the body, further weakening it, will intensify and speed up the deterioration process. When the energy is brought up to capacity, to strengthen the live cells so that they are able to fight the dead cells, the dead cells will slough off, unless the malignancy is in the final stages. The dead cells ordinarily have a tendency to disintegrate, sometimes sloughing off like strings."

Dena thought about this a few minutes, before pressing, "Then you're saying that all ailments are caused because the magnetic field doesn't pull enough energy from the air breathed into the lungs to supply the different parts of the body, and that when weaker sections are not supplied their necessary energy, abnormal function results. Why, then, does one person develop a cancer and another a heart condition?"

Mr. A replied, "This is the result of their own energy pattern. Each organ and part of the body has its own intelligence. The action and reaction and interaction, plus the individuality of the person's energy frequencies, all influence the pattern of health or ill health. There are so many facets to the energy frequencies in the operation of a body that it would be impossible to cover it all here."

Dena later told me, "Over the past sixteen years, most of his theories on the functioning of the body have been explained to me, and at first seemed very complex and far-out, but it becomes so simple when one understands the electrical energy operation of the body. Certainly his views on this are different from anything I've read or heard anywhere else, but so many unanswered questions of my profession are answered so simply by his explanations. He says, 'The body is the most sophisticated of all impulse relay machinery. It combines the systems similar to the automatic telephone, the computers, and other electronic devices. However, the body functions on human ray energy instead of the standard electrical energy. To my knowledge, standard electricity shocks the body and is not retained by it. The body will retain only human ray. Man hasn't scratched the surface of this subject yet.' "

The medical profession was beginning to sound warnings about the dangers of a high cholesterol count during Dena's school days. When she told Mr. A about the classroom discussions, he gave her a quizzical look and chuckled before replying, "Ever since I was a little boy, in listening to vibrations of the body, my instructions were that sludge was obstructing the functioning of a body; and following instructions I found that by recharging the field and then increasing the energy directly to the liver, the sludge would slough off into the bowel, and this became one of the usual procedures, because the condition is very common. Several years ago, after correcting another ailment in a man, he later returned and said, 'Hey, what did you do to me? The doctor has just rechecked me and finds that my high cholesterol has returned to normal.' I had never heard the word before and didn't know what it meant, but after three more such reports from other clients, I got a flash which told me, 'That's the sludge in the liver. That's what they're now calling cholesterol.' "

Another time Dena was sneezing and coughing when she arrived for her biweekly session with Mr. A. One of her ward patients, suffering from a ripe cold, had coughed in her face, and the medical student sighed, "I wish they'd find a cure for the common cold."

"It's got to run its course," Phil replied. "Like tuberculosis, the germs are always there, and when your energy drops below a certain level, the lowered resistance permits the germs to take over. In your case, because of direct exposure, you took on more germs than your body could handle. It's always best to neutralize this overdose before the germs can set up housekeeping."

"But how?" Dena demanded.

"Why, by doing what I've always done. I keep a bottle of hundred proof alcohol, such as vodka, handy. When I've been exposed to cold germs I put some of the alcohol on my little finger or a Q-tip, and insert it high in each nostril. I also rinse my mouth and gargle with the vodka, but I don't swallow it. Vitamin C is a form of food energy which in many cases increases resistance to colds, and cider vinegar is another. At the first hint that a cold is coming on, I take quite a bit of cider vinegar in a glass of water every hour." Dena reports that, since then, she has followed this procedure with remarkable success.

Dr. Smith says that "taking murmurs out of hearts is routine" for Mr. A. "I can hear them go, as can any other person, even with an untrained ear," she insists. "Hypertension is just one-two-three for Phil. In medical schools they teach that hypertension is incurable, but in his opinion it results from the tension delivered to the field at birth, and if the tension is released by the energy, hypertension no longer exists. I have double-checked such cases, and what he says certainly seems to be true. In some severe cases, several treatments may be required to do this, but as a rule Mr. A seems to have immediate success in reducing the blood pressure to normal."

Another case Dena checked was a woman in her seventies who had an umbilical hernia seven inches in diameter. She reports that after a series of periodic treatments "the hernia vanished, so that I couldn't even put my little finger in her navel."

I wondered aloud whether Mr. A's healing gift encompasses mental as well as physical ailments, and Dena assured me it does. She told of a woman brought in to see Mr. A, in the care of two powerful guards, who set her on a chair. Great bald patches missing where the woman had torn hunks of hair from her head gave her a weird appearance, and when she noticed a light hanging by a cord from the ceiling, she whispered, "Get rid of that dictaphone." Phil gently told her that he would do so immediately, and he unscrewed the bulb from the light socket.

"Then he began treating her magnetic field," Dena recalls, "and the woman became peaceful and relaxed. In fact, she was so calm that in ten days she was released from the mental hospital."

Impressed, I asked Mr. A how this was possible, and he responded, "Mental illness is purely and simply tension in the magnetic field. It results just from tensions in the field, like most of the other ailments."

Dena and Mr. A also related this incident to me: After Mr. A corrected the heart condition of a woman whose husband was an official at one of the state mental hospitals, Mr. A was invited to the hospital to demonstrate the energies. Skeptical of what might happen, the official said to Mr. A, "I'm from Missouri, and you'll have to show me." Apparently unconcerned, Mr. A replied, "Good. When do we start?"

"You're too eager," the man muttered, but he took Mr. A to a large room where approximately eleven patients had been stationed. Most were either restrained or with attendants. The official told Mr. A, "I'm warning you in advance, I'm not giving you any quarter. These are some of my worst cases, as you see." Mr. A smiled. "Great, I'm not asking for any quarter." Immediately he started generating the energies to the magnetic fields of the warped and confused patients, explaining to the official, as he worked on patient after patient, that according to his signals so-called mental conditions are the result of extreme tension in the field, or master brain in the pelvis, which causes the secondary pressure on the subsidiary brain in the skull.

The hospital official, who was also a state official, watched bug-eyed as Mr. A's ministrations unwound and relaxed the patients. Then he said, "Now, I just want to know one thing. What *can't* you fix?" Mr. A responded with a broad grin. "A hell of a lot of things. Let's go eat."

# CHAPTER XI

## Energy over the Air

In 1962 Dena was graduated from medical school and became Dena L. Smith, MD. She took her internship at Los Angeles County General Hospital, and one day while on the orthopedic service she took Mr. A to the airport for his return to the Bay Area, after his session in Los Angeles.

"I shall never forget that day," Dena later told me. "As we were driving along he said to me, 'This afternoon they are liable to give you the scalpel to take a leg off.' I replied with confidence, 'Not a chance. They would never let me do a case like that, especially since I'm a female. The way they feel!' Mr. A said, 'You may have a surprise. However, when it happens, I want you not to think of the case as a person. Instead, think of it as if it were the leg of a table or a piece of furniture. Don't let the emotion of what you are doing throw you.' When he said goodbye at the airport, he grinned and said, 'Good luck this afternoon.'

"Back at the hospital, I was immediately informed that the decision had been made to amputate the lower leg of an elderly patient with gangrene, whom we had been observing for several days. I thought nothing about what Mr. A had said, because it was my job to scrub in as an assistant, but in the operating room the resident surgeon suddenly handed me the scalpel, and said, 'See if you can take this leg off.' I was stunned. I certainly didn't expect them to let me do an amputation, even after Mr. A's warning. I didn't say a word but accepted the scalpel and went to work without batting an eye, following Mr. A's advice to think of the mechanics of the job rather than the patient. When the operation was over and the patient was being wheeled from the room, the resident said to me, 'You didn't seem to get disturbed or upset at having to take a man's leg off. Since you're a woman, we thought it might get to you.' I acknowledged his remark with stiff lips, inwardly grateful for the advance coaching from Mr. A."

During her internship, when it was time for Dena to apply for specialty training, Mr. A advised her to go for general surgery.

"I had always wanted to be a surgeon," Dena muses. "In fact, it was really the only specialty that fascinated me, but I knew that because I was a woman my chances of obtaining an appointment as a surgical resident were nearly nonexistent. Still, Mr. A advised me, 'Go for general surgery. You're a natural. I'd like you to get the Kaiser Foundation Hospital in San Francisco or Oakland, because you would get the experience of operating there, and not just assisting.' Reluctantly I applied for a general surgical residency there, but I was so sure it would take a miracle for me to get an appointment that I applied to about thirty hospitals in California.

"It wasn't long before I received a letter from the Surgical Department of Kaiser Foundation Hospital in San Francisco, saying they would like to have me come for an interview, that they were seriously considering my application. I could hardly wait to tell Mr. A the good news when he arrived in Los Angeles, and I waited to answer the letter until I talked to him. When I told him about it, he said, 'I'd advise you to tell them you're too busy with your internship to come for an interview.' Stunned, I said, 'Why, if I do that, I know definitely that they won't accept me, because that just isn't done. Everyone knows how important these interviews are in securing hospital appointment.' His reply was, 'Well, it's your deal, but my signals tell me this is the way to do it.'

"This time I had my opinion of him and his signals, thinking that he just wasn't comprehending the situation. But I thought for once I'd prove him wrong, and with terrible misgivings I decided to follow his advice. I telephoned the chief of surgery at the San Francisco hospital, and quaking in my boots, I told him that I was too busy with internship duties to come to San Francisco for the interview. He said he was sorry and bid me a cordial good-bye. From the tone of his voice, I figured that was it. They weren't about to take anybody sight unseen. I was annoyed with Mr. A, and I told him so. The next day, to my utter amazement, I received a wire from the chief of surgery saying that on the basis of my records and my recommendations, they were accepting me as a resident in their four-year program and were sending the contracts to be signed. The following day I received a letter for an interview at the Oakland Kaiser Foundation Hospital, and in all I turned down more than a dozen other surgical residency programs, when I hadn't even expected to get one."

Shortly afterward, the July, 1963, issue of *Cosmo-*

*politan* magazine carried a feature article, "Beauties in Medicine." It was illustrated by photographs of several young women medics, but Dena was the only one in surgical gown to be given a full-page spread. The accompanying text by Lowell Benedict said of her: "At twenty-six, Dr. Smith is one of twelve women among two hundred interns at Los Angeles County General Hospital. A five-foot six-inch blue-eyed blonde, Dr. Smith is from Redondo Beach, California, loves to swim, play tennis, make own furniture. While completing premedical work at Pomona, she gave up skiing because an accident might have absented her from school. She'll specialize in surgery, is one of few women accepted for surgical residency at Kaiser Foundation Hospital, San Francisco, which she enters soon."

While completing her internship Dena was working in the burn ward, and one Saturday during a recap session with Mr. A, he told her, "If only people would use cider vinegar on burns immediately, by soaking a towel with vinegar and leaving it on the burned area, the vinegar would neutralize the burn action of eating further into the tissues. Oil or grease, on the other hand, only feeds the burn action." This information was later to prove invaluable.

Dr. Dena L. Smith, having passed her State Board Medical Examinations with a score of 90-plus, completed her internship in June, 1963, and for the next four years took her surgical training at Kaiser Foundation Hospital in San Francisco, serving as chief resident in surgery there from 1966 to 1967. During this period, while attending a New Year's Eve celebration at the home of Mr. and Mrs. A, Dena was assisting Bea in the kitchen when Mrs. A accidentally opened the lid of a nineteen-quart pressure cooker. Immediately a wave of boiling soup poured out, saturating Bea from the waistline down, soaking her clothing and even pouring down her stockings into her shoes.

Dena says of the ghastly experience, "Phil's earlier advice flashed into my mind, and I reached for the bottle of cider vinegar, while yelling at Bea to take off her skirt. I doused her all over the burned area, and while we stripped off her stockings and shoes I kept soaking her with the vinegar. An hour later, when I was able to get her out of her panty girdle, I discovered that the vinegar had not been able to soak through the thicker portions of the girdle. On both of her thighs were four-inch-square blisters, and I knew that it was by then too late for more vinegar.

"By this time, because of the shock to her field [as Mr. A called it] Bea was having shaking chills. Phil took her out of shock by sending energy through her magnetic field. The pain vanished, and she slept. I carefully noted that her skin was not even red, except for those two angry patches which the vinegar had not reached.

"A few days later, when I dropped by to see her, I realized that those areas would have to be grafted, because they had demarcated into third-degree burns. But when I told Phil of my decision, he said, 'You think so, huh? Would you like to learn something about burns?' He sterilized his hands, and I watched with alarm as he placed four fingers of his right hand in the middle of the raw area and started generating energy directly to it. Immediately the color of the burned area changed from the yellowish pink of fatty tissue to bright red, and in a few minutes the burned flesh dried up from its weepy rawness. 'That's how you change a third-degree burn to a first-degree burn,' Phil remarked nonchalantly. 'Not only that, but by bringing the tissue energy back to the surface, it can seal itself to prevent the leakage of the vital electrolytes of the body.'

"Within three or four days, those two patches had completely healed over to normal skin. Now, years later, Bea has two neat scars on each thigh, which look like a good grafting job except that the skin is the same color and texture as the rest of her skin and has normal sensation."

I asked Dena for her reaction as she witnessed this seeming miracle, and she exclaimed, "I was flabbergasted. By that time I had had plenty of experience in diagnosing third-degree burns during my internship and residency, both as a doctor and as a surgeon. I thought grafting was the only possible solution in such a case as Bea's, but when I observed the effects of Phil's actions, I realized this could revolutionize the treatment of burns, if people could learn to handle the energies."

If other surgeons at Kaiser Foundation Hospital were setting up unusual hurdles for Dena Smith, it would not be the first time that males have tried to discourage women from pursuing a career in surgery. For reasons known best to themselves, they transferred an eighty-year-old woman from the Vallejo branch to San Francisco, where Dena was then chief resident in surgery, for the surgical removal of a malignant tumor of the colon. Vividly recalling the case on which she operated, Dena says of the woman I shall call Bertha, "She was semisenile, with generalized arteriosclerosis which was manifested in atrial fibrillation and ischemic myocardium as documented on the electrocardiograms. In short, she wasn't the best surgical risk for a major abdominal procedure. The surgery went well, however, and the tumor was resected without any apparent compromise to her cardiovascular system.

"She did well afterward, until the second postoperative day, when she suddenly went into respiratory failure and required resuscitation consisting of cardiac massage and blood pressure stimulants. She responded to these, but later that same morning she again suffered an acute episode, becoming unresponsive even though she had been maintained on a respirator by means of a tube placed in her trachea, or windpipe. Again cardiac massage was effective in resuscitation, and at least there was heart activity, but she was unresponsive to painful stimuli, the eyes were rolled backward in her head, and the pupils were dilated, although not completely. Her skin was cold, clammy, and bluish in color, while her extremities and neck were stiff. Even though her blood pressure was maintained with the aid of potent chemical stimulants, her urine output was nil, and the respirator continued to breathe for her. In short, she was moribund.

"Friday afternoon I had left the hospital to attend a conference on pediatric surgery in the East Bay and was not due to return until Saturday afternoon to resume my usual duties. It was this particular Saturday morning that Bertha developed her complications.

When I returned to the hospital about three thirty P.M., Bertha was the first patient I checked on, as she had been on my mind all day. When I stepped through the door of the intensive care unit and saw the nurse's face, I knew it was Bertha. I was stunned when I read the above account of what had happened to her, in her hospital chart. I had been so happy for her that the surgery had gone well, without apparent difficulties or blood loss, but now this! I was sick at heart. This woman was under my skin, and I realized that I had lost her.

"Then I thought of Mr. A. I suddenly wanted to call him, not for help, because I realized she was too far gone for the energy to revive her, but because he had been such an inspiration to me through the years of study and of learning the heartbreaks in dealing with suffering people. I knew he was then working in Los Angeles, and I didn't want to add to his concerns, but something told me that I should at least let him know I had lost my patient. From the telephone booth on the second floor of the hospital I placed the call. By this time it was four thirty P.M. and Bertha's condition was deteriorating rapidly. At the moment I called, Mr. A happened to be down in the garage of the building in Los Angeles, treating a person who was too ill to get out of the car, so I waited ten minutes and called again.

"When I finally reached him, I quickly sketched the events and told him that I had lost her. He said, 'What do you mean? A quitter never wins and a winner never quits,' a sentiment he'd repeatedly expressed throughout my years of training. I told him, 'No, you don't understand. She is *in extremis*. There is no hope for her.' He asked where I was in relation to Bertha's bed, and I told him it was no use, because I was on the second floor and she was in the intensive care ward on the seventh floor of the hospital, with lots of steel and concrete between us. Then he said, 'Hold the telephone receiver so that it is pointed at her and stand back, then come back on the phone in three minutes.'

"In following his instructions, I could feel my hand tingling from the energy he was generating over the telephone from Los Angeles. After three minutes he said, 'Now hold the phone tight to your ear, and I'll send a charge of energy to you.' After I did so he said, 'Now, I've loaded you with her brand of energy. Go to her and observe her condition and then place your hands on her field for five minutes. Let me know in a few hours how she is.'

"I didn't feel the stairs beneath my feet as I ran up the five flights to her room, too excited to wait for the elevator. When I entered, she was conscious and slightly moving her legs. When she looked at me in recognition, I could have kissed her. Then I placed my hands on her lower pelvis, and she seemed to move her legs and arms with more freedom. The color of her skin improved, and I wondered if I wasn't the victim of wishful thinking, until she suddenly grabbed for her endotracheal tube. I knew that it was no dream. I restrained her hands, thinking she still needed the assisted respiration, but when she protested vigorously I removed it, and she could breathe on her own. By this time the nurse had checked her blood pressure, which was the same, since she was receiving the intravenous medication for its maintenance, but when she checked her pulse she replied that it was much stronger and now regular. Then I checked it and also found that indeed it was no longer weak and thready, but strong. By this time her skin was warm and dry, and she complained of being 'damned thirsty.' She was a character, all right.

"That night I sat with Bertha. She spent a comfortable night, except for two episodes of ventricular tachycardia and some muscle spasms in her legs. Her pupils had returned to normal and she seemed mentally alert, although she didn't remember anything about the day's events. I was glad. When tested she showed a positive Babinski's sign, indicating that there had been some compromise to the cerebral circulation. The following day a repeat electrocardiogram showed new evidence of subendocardial ischemia, and that same day I gained the courage to discontinue the intravenous drugs which had been maintaining her blood pressure. After this, Bertha was making an uneventful recovery, and soon tolerating food by mouth, passing stools, and ambulating fairly well.

"By eleven days after surgery she suddenly developed acute abdominal pain and shaking chills—the day before she was to have been discharged. The nurse called me just as I was leaving the hospital for home. After examining Bertha, my heart sank, because I realized that we would have to take her to surgery immediately. Here, now, was an acutely ill eighty-year-old woman with a septic fever, and in impending shock. After making the necessary preparations to take her back to the operating room I called Mr. A, who by this time was back in the Bay Area, as I learned by calling his home. He told me to point the receiver at

Bertha and hold it there for as long as I could. Since I was calling from the telephone outside her ward room this time, nurses and interns were milling around, and even though their glances told me of their curiosity, I continued to hold the receiver pointed in Bertha's direction.

"Mr. A had not forgotten her energy code from the previous emergency, and when I thanked him and told him I was 'no quitter' this time, he chuckled and wished me luck. When I went in to recheck Bertha, the shaking chills had stopped, her pulse was slow and strong, and I felt much better about operating on her. We found a perforation of the small intestine, which accounted for her abdominal rigidity and pain, and again she withstood the surgery without event. After surgery she made an uneventful recovery, and I breathed a long sigh of relief the day that Bertha walked out of the hospital on her own. This is only one of my many, many experiences with Mr. A and the energies which he can send over the air."

Another such experience with energies sent over the air was told to me recently by Mary E. Logan, a registered nurse who lives in Santa Barbara. This is the story in her own words:

"In December 1966 I was doing private duty nursing with a woman who was about to undergo a left radical mastectomy for cancer. The patient insisted on having Mr. A present in the hospital during the surgery so that he could treat her immediately afterward to remove the shock. Otherwise, she would not consent to the surgery.

"After surgery, I was with her in the recovery room, and I became alarmed when her blood pressure became dangerously low. Knowing personally of the amazing results Mr. A obtains with the energies, I went immediately to the room where he was waiting and anxiously told him of her failing condition. He asked the direction of the recovery room in reference to the room where he waited, and as I pointed he immediately started generating the energy in that direction.

"Three or four minutes later I returned to the recovery room and was relieved to find that her blood pressure was back to normal level, and her pulse strong and full. Within fifteen minutes we were able to move her back to her private room, where Mr. A awaited. As soon as the attendants left the room, Mr. A set to work. First he placed his right hand to the patient's upper left back area, opposite the surgery, and generated energy for about half a minute. Then he placed his hand to her lower pelvic area and generated the energy there. As he did so, I started to exercise her legs, but Mr. A said to me, 'What are you trying to do, Mary?' In the same breath he told the patient, 'Bicycle your legs.'

"By this time I was amazed at how quickly the patient had become alert, and now was startled when the patient followed Mr. A's command by bicycling her legs. Next Mr. A told her to raise her left arm, and she did so immediately, with no pain. She was completely awake and smiling by this time. Then Mr. A said, 'Shall we get her on her feet, Mary?' With that, the patient sat up on the edge of the bed without any assistance. Mr. A asked if she was dizzy, and when she replied that her head was clear, he said, 'Stand up.' She did so, and he said, 'Walk.'

172

"She took four or five steps by herself, after which he said, 'Turn on a dime.' She did, and after five or six additional steps she turned again, repeating the maneuver rapidly several more times. I was so delighted with what I was witnessing that I laughingly said, 'Shall I take her home and have her telephone for the hospital bill?' Mr. A replied with a chuckle, 'Look out, Mary. You're an RN, so you have to go through the normal channels.' Well, that was the most remarkable and rapid recovery I have ever witnessed in all my forty-four years of nursing!"

Whenever she saw him, Dena always questioned Mr. A about the different aspects of surgery, and she remembers that when she first started operating, he instructed, "Always remember, Dena, all surgery is an insult to the energy mechanism of the body, so never operate unless it is absolutely necessary. You will be told that incisions heal from side to side, but my signals tell me that they shock from end to end, and it is the shock that kills patients. Therefore, the shorter incision possible to get the job done, the easier it is on the patient, and the bigger the incision, the greater the insult."

"When Mr. A says 'shock,' it is not in the terms of the usual medical definitions," Dena explains. "He is referring to any insult inflicted on the body which disturbs the normal energy patterns and hampers the normal functioning of the field.

"Throughout my training I remembered this advice," Dena says, "although I was constantly being kidded and sometimes ridiculed for my small incisions. But I noticed that before long, many of the larger

173

incisions were being abandoned in the hospital. Mr. A also told me about closing incisions, saying, 'Always measure your stitches ahead of time so that you sew a neat, even seam, and the closer your stitches are placed, within reason, the less motion there will be in the incision. The less motion, the less irritation, and this will mean quicker healing with less scar tissue.' This made sense to me, even though during our discussions he would say, 'Why ask me? I'm no surgeon.' Again I was kidded for placing so many sutures, but it proved itself many times over.

"From the beginning he instructed me in the importance of not disturbing the integrity of the nerve structures of the body, and he introduced me to a new sensitivity in dealing with the human mechanism. Once I remember calling Mr. A in Washington, D.C., as I was on my way to the operating room to remove a broken needle from the foot of a teen-aged boy. I had had experience with these cases before and knew that the preoperative X rays were notoriously erroneous when it came to finding the needle at surgery, because it had almost invariably moved an inch or more. When I told him what I was about to do, he said, 'Make your small incision one-half inch to the inside and one inch more toward the heel than you were going to cut.'

"Scrubbed and being suited up in the operating room, I remember the anesthetist saying, 'I'll bet you don't get it on the first try.' I said, 'Well, for the patient's sake, don't you hope I do?' Then, as I followed Mr. A's specific instructions, the needle was immediately beneath my incision, and I loved the grin and wink I got from the male scrub nurse as he thumbed his nose at the anesthetist."

It would seem obvious, in such cases where Mr. A had not even seen the patients, that he was drawing knowledge from a higher source.

Dena Smith told me that during her term as chief resident at Kaiser she received word from Los Angeles that her father had undergone an emergency operation for appendicitis, but that when surgeons opened his abdomen they discovered a much more critical condition. Dena telephoned Mr. A, who promptly flew with her to Los Angeles, and she says, "When we walked into Dad's hospital room, it was apparent to me that he was dying. He was ashen gray, heaving for breath, and receiving cortisone and Chloromycetin intravenously. He didn't recognize me, but Phil promptly began giving him the energies, and within fifteen minutes Dad's face was rosy and he was taking long, relaxed breaths. Four days later he walked out of the hospital and has had no further recurrence of the trouble."

Mr. A does not pretend that his method is infallible. In fact, he says his normal batting average is about nine out of ten. In many cases, success depends on patients following through, because after a few treatments they feel much better and may consider themselves well. This is their own decision, since Mr. A leaves whether they return entirely up to them.

It is probable that I fall into the category of that tenth patient, because although Mr. A has often given me quick relief from aches and pains, I have never found the time to stay in the Bay Area long enough or to go there often enough to achieve lasting results. Perhaps I was meant to write about, but not to profit from, this man's particular brand of genius, for certainly his other patients are rapturous about the results of his treatments.

Mr. A does not attempt to restore hearing after the eardrum is gone, or to remove cataracts from the eyes. Long-standing arthritis usually requires such a lengthy series of treatments to restore sufficient energy to the field and dissolve calcium deposits that many sufferers have not had the time to devote to this process. But one elderly patient told me that Mr. A's treatments formed for her a new jaw from gristle, after surgeons removed a cancerous growth from this bone. She said that she could not even open her mouth to eat, until she saw Mr. A. Others have told me of tumors magically disappearing during his ministrations.

I once asked how he knows what to do in each individual case, and he replied, "I listen to the heart to get the physical picture. The tone of the beat tells me where the trouble is, and when I get the signal from the Powers I go to work. It's very simple, really. There are thirty-six different frequencies, making numerous combinations of magnetic field control. Often the moment that a person comes toward me, his life history unfolds to me. With that knowledge, the rest is routine."

As Mr. A used to tell Dena while she was in medical school, "When you're through with all of your formal medical training, your education just begins, and that is, knowing and understanding how to handle people. Remember, each person is as individual as his fingerprints."

# CHAPTER XII

# Mr. A Goes to Washington

I first met Mr. A's wife, Bea, in April, 1972, while gathering material for this book. A lively, blue-eyed, gray-haired woman in her late fifties, she stands five feet eight inches tall and weighs one hundred and twenty-five pounds. Mr. A, incidentally, says he used to measure six feet in his stocking feet but has "shrunk a little with the years."

Bea told me that while she was managing the hotel coffee shop in Salt Lake City many years ago, she was "sickly," suffered from anemia, and had foot trouble for which the doctors wanted to operate. She smilingly recalled that during that period a bellboy told her, "Some guy around here says he's going to marry you, but he has no time to work on it now."

"I didn't know who he was talking about," Bea said, "but whoever it was, I thought he must be pretty cocky, so I gave it no further thought. But when Phil came back after visiting his family we were properly introduced, and I decided he was pretty nice. We had several dates, and when I began to hear about his strange powers, for some reason I never doubted them. They made sense to me even before the energies corrected my ailments. I had been reared a Mormon, but I guess that I wasn't a very good one because I was a heavy smoker. Phil was smoking a pipe and cigars in those days, but he said he was not going to let a habit rule him, so he stopped, and also persuaded me to quit cigarettes."

Friends of the A's arrived to drive Bea to the Valley, and I talked to them while Mr. A was giving each a quick shot of the energy. Betty, a registered nurse, told me that five years ago she had had such a bad siege of nausea and vomiting that she'd had to carry a pan around with her from bed to chairs.

"This had been going on for a year and was getting worse, despite constant consultation with doctors who, thinking it might be an early menopause, were giving me hormones and other treatments," she recalled. "I was unable to eat, and my blood tests showed anemia. Before coming to Mr. A the first time I had lost ten pounds, but after a couple of treatments from him I felt well. Then I returned to my doctor, who rechecked me and said, 'Whatever you're doing, keep doing it. Your improvement is remarkable.' A year ago I began urinating blood, and X rays revealed that I was hemorrhaging from the kidneys. The doctor put me on antibiotics, but as soon as Phil returned to the Bay Area I went to him for treatments. The bleeding immediately stopped, and when I went back to the doctor, the X rays showed no further sign of a tumor or internal hemorrhaging."

Jerry, nineteen-year-old son of the dentist whose healing is recounted in an earlier chapter, was also at the A's house for treatment. He and his mother said that at the age of six he had suffered from osteomyelitis, an infection of the bone. Recently he developed a swelling on the right shinbone, and when X rays and tests revealed a marrow abscess, he was rushed to the hospital for an operation. Mr. A was away at the time and for ten days during Jerry's hospitalization he ran a high temperature and had to be fed intravenously in order to receive potent antibiotics. Released from the hospital, he was ordered to stay on crutches for at least a month, and Jerry says he had no desire to disobey instructions, because he could put no weight on his right leg without suffering intense agony. Then Mr. A returned, and after one treatment the pain left and Jerry no longer used his crutches.

While in the Bay Area, I talked with a number of Mr. A's patients, including Mrs. Nellie Read who lives in Middletown, Lake County. She said she has been seeing Phil since the days when he had his office on Market Street in San Francisco. "He cured me of cirrhosis of the liver," she said, "and later of a lump on the skin which melted away after one treatment."

Continuing, she said, "Four or five years ago I was called back from Nevada, where I was visiting, because several doctors had told my niece that she was in the last stages of emphysema and couldn't live more than three months. Because she was so far gone, I was able to persuade her to go with me to Mr. A. At the time she couldn't carry on a conversation without stopping after two words to breathe and cough, and she was so weak that she leaned on me while we walked. He began sending the energies through her, and then told her to breathe right down to her pelvis. She actually did so, for the first time in many years. After that treatment I couldn't get a word in edgeways, because my niece talked a blue streak without any signs of a wheeze or shortness of breath. Later we took her to a different doctor, who X rayed and X rayed and finally said, 'Who says you had emphysema? There are no signs of it.' Imagine! After numerous earlier X rays and tests had shown her in the advanced stages of the disease and her doctor's pronouncement of same. Mr. A saved her life, and I can't praise him too highly. He has done wonders in this world. Incidentally, when I asked Mr. A why my niece had developed emphysema he replied that she wasn't getting her proper nerve fuel, and in this case it resulted in her condition. The field was so weak it couldn't supply enough energy back to the lungs for their normal expansion."

I called on Miss Edna Piercy of San Francisco unexpectedly, but when I asked when she had first met Mr. A, she exclaimed, "I'll never forget the date that changed my life. It was March 20, 1953. I was terribly crippled with arthritis and had been undergoing treatments with the best specialist in San Francisco for two years, but getting no better. I was loaded with hormones, was receiving injections twice a week, and living on puree and baby foods because of an ulcer. I had that moon face you get from hormones and was losing control of my legs. I was in continual pain, and the specialist told me I had both rheumatoid and osteoarthritis, with inflammation of the tissues. You can imagine how desperate I felt. I finally switched to a physical therapist at the University Hospital, who after seeing my condition said, 'Look, if you can keep it under your hat, I know a man who can help you.'

"I was medically minded, so I had extreme doubts about it, but I thought it would do no harm to try him. His jargon about 'oiling the joints' confused me at first, but I went every day because I quickly realized that I was beginning to breathe deeply again. During the second week I exclaimed, 'Look! Those swollen joints in my fingers are going down.' Then the calcium deposits in other joints began to dissolve so fast my kidneys couldn't handle it and became irritated, and then I was hospitalized; but Mr. A treated my kidneys, and the condition cleared up immediately.

"I had arthritis in my whole body: shoulders, hands, feet, hip joints. Everywhere except my spine. After the first six weeks I recognized steady improvement, but it took a year or so for Mr. A to work it completely out of my system. I had never had good health, probably due to a difficult birth, and I had had a long history of chronic allergies, but for the past sixteen years since those treatments my health has been better than it was at any other time in my life."

Miss Piercy, the daughter of a renowned chemist, who once had to give up her career as a commercial artist and wallpaper designer because of crippling arthritis, reports that she is now without a trace of it, and she looks to be in glowing health.

In Hollywood, California, I met Mrs. Isabel H. Briggs, the delightful mother of Marta Burleigh, wife of a government official, whom I had known a number of years ago in Washington, D.C. Mrs. Briggs told me that in 1957 she went to her oculist for a routine examination and pressure check on the glaucoma for which she was taking drops and that he "became alarmed and hurried me into surgery.

"I had both eyes operated on within three days," Mrs. Briggs continued. "Then something went wrong and the right eye was reoperated on the fifth day, so that I was in the hospital for three weeks, and when a friend came to be with me on my release, she exclaimed that I looked ninety. I myself was horrified at the change I saw in the mirror. Fortunately Mrs. Nell Hickman, the daughter of a doctor, arranged for me to see Mr. A, and after one treatment my friends couldn't get over the difference in my appearance. From the moment of that first treatment I began to snap back. I was in my sixties at the time. Ten years later I had a bad bout of pneumonia and afterward began to notice some difficulty with my heart. My ankles began to swell, and the doctor told me that an abdominal pressure was causing strain on my heart. In 1969 and 1970 I underwent cataract removal operations on first the right and then the left eye. Each time I was fortunate to have treatments from Mr. A after surgery, to remove the shock, and each time I recovered quickly without complication. I seemed to feel so much stronger after the treatments! My color improved, and the bothersome watering of my eye was eliminated.

"The following May I noticed that I was growing weaker. I couldn't walk from one room to another without feeling light-headed and breathless, and my heart pounded. I went to a doctor, who took an electrocardiogram and prescribed heart medicine. The friend living with me became concerned about my condition and wrote my daughter Marta that I had passing-out spells, but when Marta telephoned I didn't tell her that I was also vomiting frequently. She was living in Washington, and I didn't want to worry her, but she telephoned long-distance to my doctor, who told her, 'After all, your mother has an eighty-four-year-old heart.'

"With that, Marta telephoned Mr. A, who said he would come to Hollywood in three days to see me. I was so sick that I wanted to go to the hospital, but Marta took a plane immediately, and before she arrived I passed out again.

"As soon as Marta saw my condition, she again contacted Mr. A and told him that I had been unable to keep anything on my stomach. He told her, 'Start your mother on bonded whiskey and soda crackers, one every fifteen minutes followed by a sip of the whiskey, but be sure she chews the crackers until each is liquefied and rubbed over the roof of the mouth before swallowed.' Then Marta handed the receiver to me, and Mr. A sent a charge of energy to me over the telephone. Immediately I felt better and could breathe a little easier, and Marta said that my color improved. Then I got my crackers and whiskey, and it wasn't long until I ate a piece of apple and some bacon, which stayed down.

"The next day I stayed in bed, because I was having great difficulty in breathing and couldn't walk without assistance. My medical doctor told Marta there was an electrical problem with my heart, which was beating completely out of control. As a result, he said, it couldn't pump sufficient blood, and if I passed out again I would probably be dead. He wanted to get me into the hospital immediately, but Marta insisted on waiting for Mr. A, who arrived that evening. My skin was gray, my eyes sunken, and I was weak and gasping for breath when he came, but when he started the energy through my field I was able to breathe deeply for the first time in ages, and I actually felt the weight leave my chest. I started to yawn, and that night I slept perfectly for the first time in many long weeks.

"The next day I could feel my strength increasing with each treatment. I suddenly had a good appetite and started eating without nausea for the first time in over two weeks. By the third day my speech, which had been slurred and disjointed, was back to normal. My head cleared, and I could think again. Also, after the first day of treatments, a chronic nose congestion disappeared along with the accumulation of phlegm. Instead of the usual twenty tissues each morning, it all came up in one gob.

"For some months I had been feeling a peculiar pressure in my upper abdominal area, and when Mr. A listened to my chest he found an obstruction in the area of the liver and pancreas. He described it as dormant tissue which was deteriorating the live tissue and said that he hoped to generate enough energy into the good tissue to help it survive and to slough the dormant tissue. On the fourth day, during one of my treatments, suddenly buzzing, hissing, sizzling noises started coming from my abdomen under his fingers. Then a little later, when the right side of this area broke loose, my daughter standing across the room could hear a clacking noise coming from my tummy. Such a relief! I was no longer short of breath, and I haven't had an ache or pain since that exciting day a year ago. Before Mr. A's treatments my right hand and arm had seemed almost uncontrollable, and a business letter was returned to me as illegible, but now I can write with speed and ease. My whole body is elastic and young-feeling, and I'm a new woman at age eighty-five."

When I first saw Mrs. Briggs she was vigorously

striding across the lobby of the hotel where I was staying, and when we later chatted it was apparent that her mind was as sharp and clear as a woman half her age. Her eyes sparkled, and her body moved with youthful grace.

Marta Burleigh told me that before she met Mr. A through Nell Hickman and her mother, she had twice undergone abdominal surgery. In recent years she noticed it was increasingly difficult to stand erect, because "something seemed to be pulling my chest down; it was as though I had binding down my rib cage, and I couldn't get breath into that area." While Mr. A was treating her mother, he also sent energy through Marta, and she says, "The steel bands are now gone, my ribs are flexible, and the expansion is so much greater that I am wearing a larger bra than I have ever worn, though I am thirty pounds lighter than at my heaviest weight."

Continuing, Marta said, "I used to have a trick toe which at times hurt as though a redhot coal was being applied to it, and for years I had been going from doctor to doctor, seeking relief. Finally one day when the toe was screaming, I went to see Mr. A and he traced the nerve to the source of the trouble, finding it up under the ribs on the right side, a result of the old abdominal surgery. Though it had given me hell for fifteen years, he stopped the pain immediately when he touched the spot under my ribs, and within a short time there were no recurrences of pain."

Far more serious, however, were the physical ailments of Marta Burleigh's husband, whom I also know. A decade or so ago, during his government career, he was assigned to Bolivia where he suffered

185

keenly from the high altitude and was under severe physical strain. When he finally was due for reassignment, Marta returned to California ahead of him for a visit with her family and gave him the telephone number where she could be reached as soon as he knew which flight he would be taking. After her departure he went to a doctor, who examined him and advised that he see his own physician the minute he reached the States. On the day he was due to arrive in Miami, to change planes for Los Angeles, Marta waited by the telephone for the long-distance call to tell her which plane to meet, but none came. The plane which she thought would be his arrived, but still there was no word. Three hours later the telephone finally rang. It was her husband, who had been standing for hours on a street corner three blocks from her hotel, "numb and dazed," until he at last called a friend who reminded him where Marta was registered.

Marta rushed her husband to Mr. A, who fortunately was in Los Angeles that day, and as soon as he leaned his ear to the man's chest, he called for Dr. Smith and Marta to come and hear it. "His heart didn't sound right to me," Marta says, "but I don't understand such things. However, when I saw the look on Dr. Smith's face I knew something was sadly amiss, and under Mr. A's prodding Dena reluctantly said, 'This is the way a heart sounds under the pressure of a terminal illness.' On examination, she found the liver greatly enlarged.

"Mr. A gave my husband treatment for four days, after which he had to report to his agency in Washington and take a physical examination. He passed the physical, apparently because his health and vitality, as

186

a result of the treatments, seemed so good that there was no need to search for any problem. Then we went to our own doctor in Baltimore, who found a serious liver condition, and she was puzzled that he could look and act so well with such an ailment. We immediately flew back to California for more treatments from Mr. A, and when my husband returned to our Baltimore doctor she gave him another thorough examination before declaring that his liver was now of normal size and functioning as well as any healthy liver."

Marta Burleigh was among the friends of Mr. A who had originally urged him to add Los Angeles to his schedule. After moving to Washington, D.C., she began appealing to him to come to the nation's capital for a demonstration. One was finally scheduled in 1962, and among those present were a number of cranial osteopaths from East Coast states. Many of these medical doctors had been ailing for years with an assortment of ills which had defied specialists and each other, but one by one Phil alleviated their pain and brought them quick relief. These doctors were so delighted with the result of his ministrations that they asked Mr. A to give another demonstration, to which they brought their most difficult cases. Some of the grateful letters they later wrote him said in substance, "We brought our most baffling cases to see if they could stump you, but you are the one who stumped us."

Among those at the second demonstration was a well-known Republican member of Congress who had been hearing of Phil's unique healing method from California friends and wanted to experience it.

That legislator has since taken several series of treatments from Mr. A each year and has frankly said, "I owe my life to him."

Mr. A added Washington to his travel schedule, making six to eight trips there each year, and the enthusiastic legislator arranged for him to treat a number of Senators and other government officials. It was during one of those trips in early 1966 that Mr. A was introduced to me by Marta Burleigh and the wives of two high-ranking officials, and my personal experience with his magnetic treatments has been recounted in *A Search for the Truth*.

One of the officials whom Mr. A saw in Washington had previously consulted practically every top heart specialist in the East and had often been hospitalized in intensive care with a pacemaker, but nothing seemed to help his very irregular heartbeat, which was said to be a type of heart block. Mr. A, by using the energies, apparently corrected the heart blockage, because after two short treatments the man said that he had never felt better in his life. Later his wife told Dena Smith, "You don't know what it means to me that he now has a normal heartbeat. My life had been a terror, thinking that he might die at any moment."

A prominent registered nurse who had done private nursing in some of the wealthiest homes of America, and had written several books on childbirth, practically kidnapped Mr. A after one of his demonstrations, so determined was she that he treat some of her own patients. Phil managed to telephone Bea at one of the stops, and when she asked where he was going, he replied, "I don't know. I'm on a midnight ride with a nurse."

Dr. Dena L. Smith was in from the beginning on the case of a seventy-eight-year-old woman who, on hearing of Mr. A's successes in Washington, had her daughter bring her there from her home in New York City. She brought medical reports, revealing that she had such a severe case of diabetes that she was on sixty units of insulin a day. Her doctor had said that she had a severe heart block and that her pulse was thirty instead of the normal seventy-two. Her lips were blue, and she had frequent blackout spells, but during the first treatment with Mr. A her heart came up to normal volume, and the rate improved.

For the next two years, the woman had periodic buildups of the energy during which time she was gradually able to reduce the insulin and finally to discontinue it. On a recent birthday, her eightieth, she telephoned to report that she was feeling fine, needed no insulin whatsoever, and had had no further blackouts or distress. When her daughter also verified this, I asked Mr. A, "Don't you get a thrill when something like this happens?"

"No," he replied. "I don't even think about it. I'm just grateful to the Powers for enabling me to help people."

# CHAPTER XIII

## When a Guy Goes Fishing

Barbara and Harold Gabrielson own a resort at Orr, Minnesota, where Mr. A rented a cottage four years ago to enjoy the fishing. At the time the Gabrielsons knew nothing of the mysterious powers attributed to Phil, but after he left for home a friend told Barbara that if she wanted to know more about her recent guest she should read a chapter called "The Ancient Wisdom" in Ruth Montgomery's book, *A Search for the Truth.*

Barbara immediately procured a copy, and when Mr. A returned to Orr the following summer, the book was on the counter in the lobby. As Mr. A inquired how they were, the mother said that her shoulders were aching, and Mr. A, seeing the book, said, "Oh, have you read Chapter 17? I've heard of that man, and maybe if he were here he would just put his hand on you like this and the ache would disappear." He placed his hand on the mother's shoulder, and in a moment she said, "My pain is gone!" Then Harold Gabrielson said he had a terrific backache. Chuckling, Mr. A quipped, "Well, if that man Mr. A were here, maybe he would touch you here, like this," as he placed his hand on the man's upper chest and generated the energy. Within one minute Gabrielson could not find his backache, even with turning and twisting and trying to make it hurt. Then he exclaimed, "I've been suffering with my back for years, often awake all night with excruciating pain, and you do this for me in less than a minute. I can't believe it!"

While preparing the material for this book I talked for the first time with Barbara Gabrielson, who gave permission for me to use their names, and said that her husband's backache never did return after that one instantaneous charge of energy from Mr. A. She also told me this story:

"Five years ago I had a hysterectomy, and since then had been going back to my doctors every three months for check-ups. Last summer my head felt as if it weighed a thousand pounds, my legs were like rubber, I was trying to operate our resort at the height of the season, and my husband was preparing to leave for the Mayo Clinic because of acute heart trouble. Luckily Mr. A came again to Orr, and after he treated Harold the doctors could find nothing wrong with him, and he has had no further recurrence of heart trouble.

"At that time I had a huge stomach. I looked eight months pregnant, but after several days during which Phil sent the energies through me, my dress size dropped from a sixteen to a ten, yet I did not lose a pound. Until Phil began treating me, I knew that I was dying. I had an extensive mass in my abdomen which felt like lead, but after the first two treatments I passed two large bloody masses, and the swelling disappeared. Ever since the hysterectomy I had suffered from such horrible headaches that I was simply living on Anacin, but I have had no headaches since, and I don't take drugs anymore."

Mrs. Gabrielson said that for seven years she had also suffered from weeping eczema in the ears, and despite treatment by seven doctors and dermatologists, the condition showed no improvement. "Last fall," she continued, "my ears closed shut, my whole face was swollen from the eczema, and the pain was unbearable. Harold reached Mr. A on long-distance telephone, and under his instructions I put the receiver on my abdomen for one minute, and then to my ear. The ear opened up, and I have had one treatment since, during which Mr. A put a charge under my rib cage, and then in both ears at once to cross-fire the condition. I have had no further pain or trouble, but I go to Mr. A twice a year to keep my energy up. I feel simply marvelous!" And she looks marvelous, this trim, svelte woman from Minnesota.

Cal Ferguson of Rockford, Illinois, also likes to vacation in Minnesota during the fishing season, but while at Pelican Lake in 1969 he became ill and went to a clinic in Virginia, Minnesota. After taking X rays, the doctor diagnosed his condition as diverticulosis and prescribed medicine, but he found no relief from it. During the subsequent winter, unable to eat, he lost forty-five pounds, and felt so sick that he went to his doctor in Rockford, who took another set of X rays and found the same condition—diverticulosis.

The summer of 1970 Mr. A returned to Orr for vacation, and while there he treated Cal Ferguson at his family's request. Afterward Cal was able to eat and feel no discomfort. He gained twenty pounds and, on returning home, decided to revisit his doctor for a checkup. The physician, scarcely believing the change in his patient, asked what he had been doing, and Cal replied, "If I were to tell you, you wouldn't believe me."

"If you have time to tell me, I have the time to listen," the doctor replied, and after hearing Cal's story he declared, "Now I want to take another set of X rays just to see how things are." The new X rays were compared with the previous set. Everything in the second set showed normal, and the doctor said, "I'm happy to see this, Cal. I have heard of these treatments and know they can be successful. You are a very lucky man to have been able to see Mr. A." Cal Ferguson reports he is now back to his normal adult weight of two hundred and fifteen pounds, and feels great after only one treatment from Mr. A.

The Gabrielsons also persuaded Mr. A to treat another man, who for a number of years had had a recurrent bladder tumor which required him to be hospitalized for its removal every three months. Mr. A gave him two or three treatments with the energy, and the following year when Mr. A returned to Minnesota, the man informed him that although he continued to go to his doctor every three months, there had been no subsequent signs of the bladder tumor. Then he said, "I want to take you out fishing, particularly to Kettle Falls, but I'm not familiar enough with the underwater rocks to take my boat, and the only good pilot for the treacherous waters can't make the trip. He's had a stroke, is on crutches, and has a brace on one leg. His doctor says he's also in the last stages of emphysema." Then he added with a laugh, "But if you can fix him up, we'll have our pilot."

Mr. A replied, "Let's see the fellow." The energy was generated through him, and he began breathing deeply for the first time in years. Becoming exhilarated at the change, he tossed aside his crutches; and the next morning, at the controls of his own launch, he took the group to Kettle Falls. Friends report that since then the man has been able to navigate stairs without difficulty, either with his walking or his breathing.

On that same trip, the family of a seventy-seven-year-old woman who owned a resort lodge asked Mr. A to help her. "She had the death rattle, and her lungs were full of fluid," a friend told me later. "She also had a large knee joint that had been frozen solid for fifty years. When Mr. A generated the energy current through her field, her lungs opened immediately. She breathed freely and by the next morning had used fourteen boxes of Kleenex to contain the eliminated fluid. The elderly woman, a one-time chorus girl, then began flexing her knee and swinging it over a chair, after Mr. A had cross-fired the energy into the frozen joint. Until that day the woman had had three or four bouts of pneumonia every winter, but for four years since Mr. A's treatments there has been no recurrence of pneumonia, and she hasn't stopped showing off her knee motion. She really gets around!"

Mr. A, who had been listening with twinkling eyes to these accounts, chuckled. "When a guy wants to go fishing, it's hell what he has to do."

Another of Mr. A's patients is Robert Roy Goodell of Santa Monica, California, who is a rehabilitation counselor for the Veterans Administration. At age sixty-one he is the picture of health, belongs to two sports clubs, and is an avid enthusiast of figure skating, jogging, and swimming. While talking with me recently in California, he told me, "There is no question in my mind but that Phil saved my life. In 1966, while working at McDonald Douglas Aircraft, I suffered a heart attack. Company doctors said my blood pressure was 220, my pulse was highly elevated, and I was suffering acute pains in my chest and down my arm. They called in a heart specialist who, after taking a cardiogram and making other tests, said I needed immediate hospitalization and would be off work for at least twelve weeks, perhaps a year. Fortunately for me, Mr. A came to Los Angeles before they could get me into the hospital, and he gave me a few treatments. A couple of days later I returned to the doctors, who made a cardiogram both before and after a fatigue test consisting of stepping up and down a three-step 'pigstile,' I call it, thirty-two times within three minutes. The cardiologist expressed surprise at my control in returning to even and normal breathing, but said he would withhold further comment until all tests were completed at St. John's Hospital, including blood tests, kidney tests, and X rays.

"I felt tremendously vibrant and full of life, so I was not worried about the upcoming tests, but the consultant cardiologist really went all out, with full blood test, double masters fatigue test, renogram kidney test with isotype tracer, the IVP rapid method series of ten X rays after injection into the blood of a radioactive tracer, a kidney and bladder test, four X-ray views of the heart after I had swallowed barium, the treadmill fatigue tests, more blood tests and a lot of cardiograms.

"Much to my doctors' amazement, the T-waves in the cardiograms had returned to normal, and I passed everything except one fatigue test. I had a few more treatments from Phil, after which the company doctors sent me back to work, eleven weeks ahead of schedule, and I have had no trouble since. But just to be on the safe side, I see Mr. A for a recharge three or four times a year. Recently I noticed a thyroid nodule on my neck, and since Phil was away I went to a specialist who gave me scanning X rays, which showed up a lump the size of an English walnut. He prescribed five grains of thyroid a day, but after Mr. A returned and treated it, the lump disappeared."

I happened to be present recently when Mrs. Dorothy Traube of Belleville, Illinois, met Mr. A for the first time. She told us that thirty years ago she had had an operation for removal of her gall bladder, "and I haven't felt right since. I have neck trouble, pressure on the head, and the doctor says my heart is skipping beats. I've been greatly bothered by adhesions and scar tissue since the operation and have never been free of abdominal pain."

Mr. A put his ear to her chest, and then began sending the energy through her abdominal area. Immediately her heartbeat became regular, and after several more treatments she told me, "I feel fine now. The scarred area has softened so that I am no longer bothered by the pressure or the pain, and I've had immediate relief from long-standing sinus trouble and tennis elbow as well."

Patients ordinarily go to Mr. A for one particular, over-riding ailment, but they soon learn to tell him about every other ache or pain, because in his engaging way, he says with a grin, "You point it and I'll shoot it. Fair enough?"

In preparing this book I met for the first time Olive Stuart, the opera singer from Phoenix referred to in a previous chapter. She told me she had suffered a ruptured appendix in childhood, "which left a horrible scar and weakened me physically."

The attractive, vivacious woman continued, "I had been sickly most of my life with asthma, colds, and total exhaustion. Doctors were constantly giving me pills, to no effect. One day, standing on a sidewalk, I became very ill and began praying for guidance. Within a week Mrs. Hickman told me about a miracle man in San Francisco, and although I didn't believe it, I was so deperate that I flew up there. The moment I saw Phil, he looked like electricity to me. I don't know any other way to describe it. I was terribly sick, but after he began the treatments I did nothing for three days but go to the toilet, and sleep. He was washing the toxins right out of my system, as he opened my circuits and rebuilt my depleted field. Until then I had been taking five Tedral tablets a day for asthma, to dilate my bronchial tubes, but I have never needed them since. I am a well woman, but if I feel tension building up, I call Mr. A when he is here in Los Angeles where we now live."

I also talked with Olive's husband, Leslie Stuart, who at the time of their first meeting with Mr. A was stage manager for the Hollywood Bowl and production stage manager for the Pilgrimage Theater, which each summer presents the story of Christ. He later became director of the Phoenix Civic Light Opera Company and in now supervisor of the Van Nuys branch of the Los Angeles Municipal Court. He described how Mr. A had removed his "kinks, aches, and pains," and then told me two shaggy-dog stories which he and Olive swear are literally true. This is their report:

They have two mixed terriers, Rocky and Beegee. One morning Rocky came home with his high-curled tail limply hanging down. He slid under the bed, yelping pathetically, and they rushed him to a veterinarian, who gave him a tranquilizer and then found that he had broken bones near the base of his tail. The vet kept him for a week, and when the Stuarts took Rocky home he told them, "There's nothing I can do about the tail. He'll never wag it again." Luckily Mr. A came to town, and he fired the energy through the animal's chest. Mr. Stuart said that Rocky slept for three days. "Then he came on like Gangbusters, with his tail up, and has continued to wag it ever since."

"Later Beegee developed troubles," he continued, "and the vet said he would have to perform a hysterectomy. We tried to telephone Phil long distance, but he was away, so Beegee had the operation. When we brought her home she lay flat on her back, too stiff to move. After numerous attempts they located Phil who was in Washington, D.C., and he told them to put the receiver on her incision for a minute, while he sent the energies through her. You would have had to see it to believe it. Immediately afterward she began racing around the house like a playful puppy and has had no further problems."

I asked the Stuarts about the demonstration which Mr. A gave several years earlier at their home in Phoenix, and Olive prompted, "Tell her about our friend Don, who had mononucleosis." Chuckling reminiscently, Leslie Stuart said, "Yes, when Phil blasted the energy to Don, who was in his thirties, an older man sitting behind Don turned deathly white and fainted. He was in the line of fire."

The next time that I saw Mr. A I asked him about this unusual occurrence, and he replied, "The man in front of me was not easy to treat, requiring a high potency of the energy to handle his ailment. Over the years I've found that most people are easy to treat and will feel the current of energy generated, but approximately three out of ten will not feel it, although they still get the results as if they did. In this particular case, the charge of energy necessary to blast this man was incompatible to the older man behind him, and his field could not handle this potency of opposing current." The man quickly recovered and was none the worse for wear.

Rose Goodspeed of San Francisco told me that while operating a real estate business in Cambria Pines, California, twenty-five years ago, she suffered a massive heart attack. "I couldn't breathe or speak," she says, "and while in the hospital the heart specialist said that I might live a year if I was careful. Needless to say, I was pretty despondent. Then someone told me about Mr. A, and all hunched over, I went to see him. He started working on my legs and under my left little toe, sending the energies. After fifteen minutes he put his fingers near my lower ribs, and suddenly I could breathe freely and straighten up. After five such treatments in two weeks I went back to my doctor, who rechecked me and exclaimed, 'It just can't be! It never happens like that.' I was well.

"Much later, in 1960, I went through a cancer detection clinic, and when the reports were in, the gynecologist sent for me to say that I had cancer of the cervix and must go into the hospital that evening. I refused and went instead to Mr. A for treatments. Three months later I returned to the gynecologist, and although he grumbled about my earlier refusal to be hospitalized, he ran the tests on me again. This time his report was that all traces of the cancer had vanished. I've now celebrated my eightieth birthday and am still going strong."

While sitting in Mr. A's outer office, I spoke with a number of his patients before and after their treatments. One was Charles E. Emmerson of Arcadia, California, sales supervisor for Featherrock, Inc. He said that he first heard about Mr. A in 1955 while in Virginia, and that when he returned to California he looked him up, "because nerves from old surgery were causing me to favor the right leg.

"After one treatment from Mr. A, it hurt worse," he continued, "but I had another treatment the same day, and from that point on I walked like I used to before the original problem arose. Four years ago I was hospitalized because of an automobile accident. I had a large hemotoma covering the entire surface of my left forearm, but after a few treatments from Mr. A my doctors were baffled by how rapidly it had vanished. My wife Frieda had a broken rib which showed up on X rays, and it was exceedingly painful, but with two treatments from Mr. A she suffered no further discomfort.

"Last year, during my annual physical checkup, X

201

rays and an intravenous pyelogram revealed a kidney tumor, and I was informed that I would have to have surgery as quickly as possible. Instead I went for two treatments from Mr. A, and the next day returned to the doctor for a renotomogram, X rays of every level of the kidney. Miraculously, they could find no trace of the tumor."

Viola Allee, a sweet faced, gentle woman, told me that until twelve years ago she was in constant misery because of leg and back trouble and her doctor said she must live on cortisone the rest of her life. Then someone told her about Mr. A, and when he listened to her chest he said that her problems stemmed from the shock of a dry birth. She was astonished, but on checking with her mother she learned that it was indeed true. She took treatments from Phil periodically for two or three years, and now says, "I regularly climb twelve-thousand-foot mountains in south Utah without any discomfort, and I've had no problems since the treatments, although I come in occasionally to receive the energy, to keep fit."

Some years ago, Viola Allee worked with a group of subnormal children, two of whom were mongoloids, in a Catholic Day School in Santa Barbara. Thus, when a friend who was a music teacher gave birth to a baby girl, Viola recognized almost immediately that she was mongoloid. Not until eighteen months later did the child's mother realize the condition, and then she resolved to rear Alice herself, instead of institutionalizing her. Ten years ago, when Alice was fourteen, she could not talk intelligibly or read. She had a shapeless figure with ungainly hips and thighs, but

Mrs. Allee brought her to Mr. A, and after a year or two of periodic treatments, Alice was able to talk intelligently and clearly.

"Alice now thinks and reasons, and is quite sharp mentally," Mrs. Allee told me. "Not only that, but after she started the treatments her body became more streamlined, and she is very concerned about her appearance. Now, at twenty-four, she enjoys good health and is able to work for compensation. I have since learned that when mongolism is recognized early, and these infants are brought for energy from Mr. A, the results are absolutely amazing."

One of the most charming women to whom I talked in Mr. A's outer office was introduced to me as Bea Harding. During our conversation I learned that she is the widow of John "Jack" Harding III, the famed aviator who in 1924 piloted one of the four "world cruisers" which set off to fly around the globe. One of the four planes was forced down and returned to this country by warship. Another was lost in Alaska, but Jack's plane and one other completed the historic mission, traversing 27,553 miles of arctic and tropic ocean, glacier and forested peaks, desert and jungle in one hundred and seventy-five days. Jack Harding was born in 1896 near Nashville, Tennessee, at Belle Meade, a 5,000-acre plantation which had been owned by his family for four generations. Following his world flight, he joined commentator Lowell Thomas on a lecture tour that took them into every state of the Union. Then Jack flew the mail in Florida with Eddie Rickenbacker, and after marrying Bea he joined the Boeing Aircraft Corporation in California. The Hardings occupied a penthouse apartment in La Jolla overlooking the sea, but in 1968 he died of cancer.

Not long afterward Bea developed a serious condition, and when a friend told her about the miracle man in San Francisco, she went to see him. This is the way Mrs. Harding recalls her experience: "There was a solid hard mass in my abdomen, but after a few treatments I began passing bubbly strings in the urine, and the bloat and hardness disappeared. Doctors pronounced me cured, and when I revisited Mr. A for a checkup last November, before he left for his winter vacation, he told me to stop smoking because of my lungs. I was a chain smoker, and had been for years.

"In December I fell, spraining my ankle and hitting my spine very hard. From that day on, I didn't feel a bit good and kept feeling worse by the day. About three months later I went to my internist for a complete physical examination and tests, and when he gave me a complete bill of health it occurred to me he hadn't ordered a chest X ray. Remembering what Mr. A had said about my lungs and smoking, I requested one, and after studying my X rays the doctors insisted on a lung biopsy, because they saw a small blemish.

"Since Mr. A was unavailable, I had to permit the surgery, during which they removed the middle lobe of my right lung. One week later Mr. A returned to California, and when I went to see him my heart was under maximum strain, totally irregular in beat. Doctors said that my heart was in atrial fibrillation, and also the scar tissue in my chest incision was a half inch thick. I couldn't get my breath, because I felt like a rope was tied around my chest. After three minutes of treatment by Mr. A, the heartbeat was controlled and regular, and I could breathe deeply. After additional treatments that day and the next, the scar tissue became so soft and thin that my scar barely showed, and the rope-feeling was completely released. Mr. A is a marvel! If only I had known about him in time to save Jack's life."

Manly P. Hall, accompanied by his wife Maria, also came into the office for a periodic buildup treatment and for a game of Chinese checkers with his friend Phil. In reminiscing, Mrs. Hall told me of the memorable day in 1951 when she met Mr. A. "It was my first time in Phil's office, and I was exceedingly skeptical about the wonders I had heard attributed to his powers. While awaiting Manly's turn, two people brought an old man in on a stretcher. He was terribly crippled with arthritis. His fingers were curled into his hands, and his hands into his arms like claws. A short time later the old man walked out of the inner office and stood wide-eyed, staring at his open palms. They had seemingly returned to normal, and he left on his own two feet. I couldn't believe my eyes."

Manly Hall continued: In 1963 I had been sick in bed with a gall bladder attack, and for several days had been unable to get out of bed. My abdomen was distended, and I was vomiting green bile. The doctors told me I was too overweight to risk the necessary operation, and I was really sick. Maria called Phil, who was working in Los Angeles at the time, and he came to my home. After greeting me, he said, 'Well, Manly, looks like you're in trouble, so we'll see what the energies will do. Otherwise I know they'll pick me as a pallbearer, and you're too damned heavy to carry.'

Phil and I are always kidding each other, but that time I was too sick even to grin. He blasted the energy through me, and soon I was back on my feet."

Mrs. Gardner W. Carr of La Jolla, California, invited Mr. A to give a demonstration of the energies for the La Jolla Edgar Cayce Study Group, and afterward she asked him for treatment. "I was desperate," she told me, "because my doctor said that my right kidney was deteriorating badly, and I must have an immediate operation. I was in excruciating pain with my kidneys when I saw Mr. A, but after the first round of treatments I had no more pain and haven't to this day. I went back to my doctor for a routine X ray, and he was greatly surprised at how my kidney was rebuilding. The second year afterward I had another X ray, but no more are needed, because I am now fine.

"A few months after my treatments with Mr. A, I took a young friend in her thirties to see him. This was difficult to do, because she was bedridden with a bad heart condition, and three doctors had given her up. Since that session she has been in buoyant health, has started a new life, and is now a teacher in Hawaii."

# CHAPTER XIV

# Diet and Foods

During my numerous encounters with Mr. A since our first meeting in 1966, I have observed his unusual eating habits. He travels with an electric skillet and special foods wherever he goes, so that he can avoid restaurants and have his own meals prepared. He even carries frozen meats and other delicacies, renting a room or suite with a refrigerator in order to preserve them until time for consumption. I had marked this down as an eccentricity until, while preparing this book, I put good manners aside and asked for an explanation. His reply proved so interesting that I consider it a vital part of his story.

"Before World War II," he began, "I enjoyed food, whether traveling or at home, provided it was properly prepared. But afterwards I increasingly found that there were foods I could not handle. My signals and my stomach told me that our food was gradually becoming so loaded with preservatives and chemicals, and later hormones, that most of it was not fit for human consumption, as far as I'm concerned. Fortunately I have a trigger stomach, and any time I happen to get an adulterated food, my stomach refuses it, and up it comes within ten minutes, before it can do harm to the body."

I asked how he manages to avoid such foods, and he replied, "In order to get meat I can eat, I buy it on the hoof, back in the hills where there's no chance the cattle have been eating grass which has been sprayed with DDT or other pesticides, and where I can be sure they've not been fed hormones or injected with them for fast fattening and fast profit. Then the meat, after proper aging, is cut and packed under my supervision, and fast-frozen so that I have a year's supply. When I'm traveling, I take along a frozen roast or other cuts which Bea has cooked in advance."

I asked why preservatives and hormones fed to cattle are harmful, and he replied, "Any preservative in food is like an embalming fluid, and I don't want my body distorted with any adulterated or synthetic food. Preservatives dormantize the tissue, which can lead to malignancy, according to my signals. Several years back, I started warning people about this. Hormones are given cattle to put weight on them and increase their worth in the marketplace, but in my opinion this dormantizes their tissue, and since I don't want the same reaction to occur in my body, I don't eat it. Years back I used to enjoy Chinese food in restaurants, but for some time now, since the chemical flavor enhancer has been added to this kind of food, my stomach won't handle it, and I have to prepare my own Chinese dishes.

"Another problem is chickens, and the eggs laid by hens who have been fed hormones. My stomach cannot handle eggs or chicken unless the chickens have been scratching on the ground and are grain fed, without antibiotics or other drugs. I refuse to eat chickens (or their eggs) that have been fed any of the high-potency feeds, known as grower feeds. Sometimes when I eat at the house of a friend who has assured me that everything served is organically grown, the host or hostess can fool me, but they can't fool my stomach. Within ten minutes up it comes if it's not right.

"Life was a great deal simpler for me before World War II, when I could travel widely and eat uncontaminated food. Nowadays I won't eat in restaurants because I can't be sure of decent food, so I take along an electric frying pan to handle the frozen meats, take bread which Bea has baked, and try to get vegetables which are authentically organic-grown. If they're not, up they come. For the same reason, I drink only raw milk whose source I know.

"I never use margarine—only butter with whose source I am familiar, and the only other fat I consider safe for me is peanut oil. These so-called vegetable oils just won't stay down. I never drink tap water anymore because of the chemicals that have been added to it. Both at home and on our travels we buy bottled springwater. I always used to feel there were sufficient vitamins in a well-rounded diet for the body's requirements, but so many things have been done to food since the war that some vitamin supplements may be necessary."

Bea, Dena, and their friends say that Mr. A is a marvelous cook, who prepares delectable concoctions seasoned for an epicure's palate. He also is said to generate energy to the food, which improves the flavor and tenderizes the meat.

Dena, who admits to a passion for home-grown tomatoes, once set out a few plants in the garden at

Mr. and Mrs. A's house, and she says of the experience, "Every time that I dropped by I inspected them hopefully, becoming more and more discouraged with their progress. Then Phil bought four plants, setting them out next to mine, and said laughingly, 'Now watch these plants grow.' As he planted each one he put the energy into it, and I shall never forget that summer. Mine remained thin and spindly, but the ones Phil set out grew so big that they resembled small trees, with big sturdy stalks, and they were simply overburdened with huge, delicious tomatoes."

Bea took up the story. "Let me tell you about the pansies. Shortly after Phil and I were married, he brought home two flats of pansies, and I wanted to plant them in one place, but he said he'd like them better in another. The exposure was identical, and both areas received equal amounts of sun. We finally settled the argument by dividing the flats in half. I planted mine where I wanted them, and he set out the rest, but what I didn't realize then was that he was buzzing each of his as he planted it. In a short while mine were flourishing like any normal pansy, but each of Phil's was like a bush, with thick, fourteen-inch-high stalks, and his pansies measured four inches in diameter. The neighbors couldn't believe their eyes!"

Dena suddenly began to laugh, saying, "I must tell you about another incident which, even if I hadn't already observed Phil's amazing healing powers with people, would have convinced me he has a gift the rest of us lack. Bea was raving about how tender and delicious their beef was, because Phil buzzed it before she cooked it, and I said, 'This I've got to see,' so we decided to cook two identical steaks side by side to test it. Before we cooked one steak, Phil put his fingers on it and buzzed the meat to tenderize it. Then we put both in the same broiler, turned them and lifted them at the same time. One was admittedly tough, but the one he had buzzed was as tender as the finest steak available anywhere."

Aware that many Oriental seers and sages who manifest strange healing powers forego the eating of flesh, I asked Mr. A for his opinion, and he replied, "The body needs a certain amount of meat for tissue building, but I do not eat a large quantity of it." Incidentally, Phil at seventy-seven has all his own teeth, which are even, white, and glistening.

I asked Mr. A whether he was able to use the strange energies to help himself, and Dena exclaimed, "He can even send that energy through his teeth. One day a heavy woman started to fall, and Phil put out his left hand to catch her; but she grabbed his thumb, bending it out of joint and breaking the bone structure around it. His thumb was lying back against his arm, but he quickly pulled it back into place. His office was full of people awaiting his ministrations, so throughout the remainder of the day, while generating energy to patients with his right hand, he held the thumb of his left hand between his teeth. By evening the energies had completely healed it."

Mr. A says that when a person's energy is up to normal it keeps the body supple, the skin soft, the bones flexible, and the teeth deterioration-free. The body needs food energy plus life energy to maintain proper body function, according to Phil, who says, "Thus, it is very important that one not only receive the properly blended mating fuel, but also that the food energy in the food one eats is not distorted. My signals since boyhood have explained that people could perhaps better maintain their optimal energy levels if the energy of the seasons were recognized."

I asked what he meant by that, and he continued, "Simply this. The twenty-first of June is the highest point of energy in the Northern Hemisphere, and the twenty-first of December is the lowest. The reverse, of course, is true in the Southern Hemisphere. It is in this low-energy period, especially felt here in November, December, January, and February, that resistance to illness drops and people are most apt to develop ailments. When the sap is going down in the trees, the energy is going down in people, and when the sap is rising in the trees, we are aware of our own rising energies. My flashes have told me that the time will come on this planet when people from the north will feed, so to speak, those in the Southern Hemisphere, and vice versa, during each other's high-energy season, by generating and radiating energy to each other. We will also learn to study the astrological patterns of ourselves and the persons with whom we are contemplating marriage, to prevent mismating energy patterns. We are only beginning to tap the lost wisdom of what life energy can do in this universe."

For as long as he can remember, Mr. A has been warning people against sunbathing, saying that skin cancer and depletion can result. At the time that Dena first met him, she was a sun worshiper who loved to tan at her parents' house at the beach. Mr. A told her one day, "Dena, if the sun pulls water out of lakes and streams, what do you think it does to your body? If clothed, a person exposed to it receives energy. Otherwise it causes dehydration and depletion of energy in people exposed to its rays."

While still in premed, Dena spent a weekend at the beach, and after swimming she lay on the sand for twenty minutes to maintain her tan. When she returned to the house, she said that she felt unwell and, instead of being relaxed, was nervous and jumpy. That evening she went to Mr. A for a treatment, and when he listened to her chest he remarked, "You must have been out in the sun."

"Only for twenty minutes," she protested.

"Yes," he replied quietly, "but that was long enough for the sun to sap your energy."

There is no end to the fascinating theories that seem to flow effortlessly from the fountain within this remarkable man. He says, for instance, that many cases of alleged heart attacks are actually gas attacks from various causes, including tension, improper food, and nerve deficiency.

I asked him about the cause of senility, and he instantly replied, "Starvation of the magnetic field is starvation of the brain. If the natural mating energies are kept up to capacity, the field can supply the necessary energy to keep the subsidiary brain alert, eliminating the slowing down of the brain as well as the body aging, which occurs over the years. If the field doesn't receive its energies, this gradually results in childishness and senility."

I looked questioningly at Dena, who nodded. "Mr. A told me that while I was in medical school," she said, "and subsequently I was able to observe a number of elderly persons who were usually brought to Mr. A by members of their families. After receiving the energies, it was remarkable to see how their reasoning and alertness improved, and how enthusiastic they became about things that had previously failed to hold their interest."

# CHAPTER XV

# The Philosophy of Living

Mr. A has tremendous respect for all life, which embraces birds, fish, humans, and other animals. He seems to have a phenomenal ability to "tune in" to animals, and he says of them, "Animals understand the generation of energy and use it when necessary. Have you ever walked into a barn in freezing weather and noticed how warm it feels? This is because the horses and cows know how to generate energy and throw off the surplus. Seldom will an animal perish from the cold, but human beings will, because man does not know enough to start the generation to keep himself warm, although in ancient days he was capable of doing so, and it was common practice for survival.

"Animals communicate with each other by waves. The undomesticated ones seek their own mates, instinctively selecting one with whom their own energy current is properly blended. They can also sense our minds, understanding our spoken word by the vibratory sound, and thus familiarize themselves with what we mean by it. Some say that a dog knows or accepts a person by scent, but it isn't simply that. It is the generation of the individual wavelength he recognizes. A dog will obey instructions given him by thought wave. The fox is so intelligent that he not only can read a person's mind, he also has unusual reasoning power. It is only humans who seem to have lost the key, but mental wave vibrations can be used as a method of communication, as science is beginning to discover. Between two people of compatible signs this art can become highly developed."

Mr. A is confident that all of us are born with this knowledge. It is only through so-called civilization and education that we lose the power. For example: A nurse who worked with Mr. A when he conducted regular office hours recalls the first spastic she saw him "release." She says of that eventful day, a long time ago, "The baby was fifteen months old, and the mother said she had taken her to numerous doctors, whose only thread of hope was that she might eventually outgrow this condition. The baby's legs were straight and rigid, and her head rolled about grotesquely. She had never held it up. We placed her on the desk while Mr. A put his fingers over the lower abdomen and directed the energy current through her for a few minutes.

"Her little legs relaxed, came up and kicked the air, and the fists unclenched as she made spontaneous baby gestures. Mr. A told the mother to hold the baby in a sitting position, and as he placed his hand on the lower spine, he said to the infant, 'Now, raise your head. That's the way. Hold it up. Fine, now doesn't that feel better?' The head wobbled, jerked a few times, then slowly came to a normal upright position in obedience to his words. The mother poured out a torrent of thanks, and after they left I turned to Mr. A, saying, 'That baby was not old enough to understand the words you spoke, but she did just as you told her.'

216

"With a happy smile, he responded, 'No, she didn't understand the words, but her nerves responded to the command of the energy in the vibrations of my voice.'

"The next spastic baby was only a year old, but she also obeyed his commands, stretched out her legs, opened her fists, and raised her head to a normal position for the first time by herself. When Mr. A placed his fingers on the infant's lower abdomen over her magnetic field, he relaxed and strengthened it, enabling it to draw more energy from the lungs. As the energy current traveled through the relays in the subsidiary brain and back, the current was established."

When I questioned Phil about the episodes, he said, "The life-force is of human ray energy, so the body must be mechanically constructed to conduct, transmit, and be activated by the human energy current. Thought control, thought direction, and discrimination are some of the many energy impulses. The individual's energy of the magnetic field, drawn from the numerous energies in the air we breathe, supplies the subsidiary brain within the skull, and all organs of the body and relay centers—the entire human structure—making each person a unique individual mechanism. This energy action and reaction on all intelligence centers of the body is Life."

I asked Mr. A about his general philosophy, and he replied, "We must respect the body as an individual planet. No person should try to own another. We should assign ourselves to assist and to help one another, but never try to own or possess. Jealousy is a deadly disease which disintegrates the body. There should be an open hand for all. Each person should be free to operate his own planet, unbound by any strings. Where jealousy enters, anger follows, and anger and fear are the two deadliest enemies to our human mechanism, causing the tension which limits the energy from the lungs to the magnetic field.

"I believe in 'live and let live.' What you send out, whether in thought or action (what I call the Law of Average) comes back to you. Ego is also a deadly thing, because you level yourself. Once you are full of self-satisfaction and think you have all the answers, you close yourself off from receiving wisdom from the magnetic Ring."

I asked Mr. A about religion, and he replied, "My instructions are that the church is within. Each person is responsible to the Power of Powers through the Law of Average. The highest universal wealth is to be contented and to be at peace within yourself. The more contented one is, the more relaxed, and the more the mind can then tune to the wisdom from the magnetic Ring and the Power of Powers. And the more wisdom one has, the easier life is, because what people understand they do not fear. Wisdom you are born with, education you must acquire. Wisdom can be dampened and distorted by education. Unless we have a clear field at birth, or unless the birth shock is released, we must rely solely on education."

Questioned about the Biblical heaven and hell, Mr. A said, "From what I get from the Powers, heaven and hell are right here while we're living. I'm told that one out of every ten people are born to give the other nine trouble, but if we have the wisdom to recognize them, we can sidestep these troublemakers. As a boy, I was instructed that the so-called Tidings of ancient times were to spend ten percent of one's time receiving wisdom from those more advanced than ourselves, and another ten percent giving their wisdom and knowledge to those with less than ourselves. We must reach for the higher and give to the lower, according to our level of wisdom.

"If everyone were doing this, people wouldn't be impairing their health by trying to outmaneuver each other on the present monetary basis, or in any other way. This would keep the human cycle closer to the natural cycles of the universe. As you sow, so shall you reap. The greatest wealth is contentment within, and to maintain it we must work at it."

I wanted to know about the newly established Life Energies Research Foundation, and Mr. A responded, "The purpose is to broaden the research into the human ray energies and their effect on our bodies and lives, and it is also designed to combine our present medical and surgical knowledge with the Ancient Wisdoms that have been virtually lost. A part of its work will be a re-education program, teaching people how to help themselves and each other, through a greater understanding of the energies."

As I understand it, Life Energies Research is to be an educational foundation which will also research Mr. A's methods and work. Phil, in discussing it, remarked, "We haven't even scratched the surface yet on the power of life energies, and what can be done with them. The Power travels in split seconds around the world and is available to anyone who is capable of receiving and handling it. For instance, my daughter at the age of five could do anything that I could with the energies. She also was born with a star in her right palm, but after neglecting the power for most of her life, one of the prongs of the star began moving away, and now is so spread that the star is scarcely discernible."

Be that as it may, his daughter is a beautiful, slender, astonishingly young-looking woman to have a new grandchild.

Dr. Dena L. Smith, who is the medical director of the foundation, told me, "I have always marveled at the speed with which Mr. A can effect changes in the body. It is usually a matter of seconds. But he says that the easy part of generating the energies is the obtaining of immediate result—grandstanding, as he calls it—but that the *real* skill is to build the mechanism to hold the correction.

"I am staggered by the great skill that is required for him to blend the energies so that the frequency, wavelengths, and complementary energy are delivered to make the corrections of the condition. Even after all my years of observation, I am unable to do what he does, but I have wanted to learn, and I have long been researching him and his work, because I felt that I could do more for more people by translating him to them. What I have learned from him has been invaluable to me in my work.

"I originally went into medicine to help humanity in my small way, but I now feel that I can be of greater service to humanity by furthering the research and documenting the effects of the human ray energy on the mechanisms of the body, especially in preventing illness before it starts."

Dr. Smith says that in observing Mr. A with his patients over the years, she has been impressed by the fact that no matter how criticial or drastic a situation may be, he never gets excited or perturbed. Instead, he exhibits a complete confidence that she has never witnessed elsewhere, and when she once asked him about this unusual quality, he replied, "Why should I get concerned? The energies will handle it."

Dena reminds that Mr. A has no hospital or clinic to help bear his burden; yet he usually gets the cases that doctors have given up on. She says that he takes those often-hopeless cases, "and within ten minutes puts them on their feet again." Yet, on this critical firing line, she has never seen him nervous or concerned.

I asked Mr. A how it feels to treat so many sufferers who come to him as their final hope, after medical science has exhausted its resources, and he replied with a shrug, "My life isn't supposed to be easy. I've always known that."

Hopefully, I asked Mr. A if he would direct the new foundation, and he replied, "No, that is a job for others. I'm willing to assist the foundation, but I'm retiring now, and not looking for more work. It's up to the people whether they want it or not."

His words somehow reminded me of the much-quoted Biblical injunction, "Ask, and it shall be given you; seek, and ye shall find; knock, and it shall be opened unto you."

Nonetheless, I implore my readers not to ask "it" of me. Mr. A chooses to remain anonymous for two excellent reasons. At the age of seventy-seven, having earned the right to retire from active duty, he would not be able to handle such a tremendously increased caseload, and he has been told by the Powers not to seek personal glorification. I am pledged not to intercede with him in behalf of those seeking cures, and because my chapter about him in *A Search for the Truth* has already produced many thousands of requests for his services, I can no longer attempt to answer the letters.

My publishers had long been urging me to write a complete book about this strangely gifted man, but I could not bring myself to do so, because there was no one to whom I could direct the deluge of mail. Having had no experience as a doctor or nurse, I was unaccustomed to knowing at close hand of the desperate ailments which beset mankind. Thus, my heart would bleed over nearly every case outlined in the letters; yet I was powerless to do other than tell my hapless correspondents that Mr. A was still anonymous.

Now, however, a foundation has been launched, and all queries concerning Mr. A should be addressed to Life Energies Research, Suite 406, 3808 Riverside Drive, Burbank, California 91505. Mr. A himself will not be available for individual treatments, but let us hope that the day will come when many other gifted persons, with superabundant energies and the ability to tune in on the Powers, will be able to duplicate the magical feats of this talented man.

Dena Smith says of the material assembled here, "This is a mere sample of the tremendous range of Mr. A's wisdom, since he has access to unlimited wisdom. The work of the foundation will be in researching and expanding this knowledge."

In conversation, Mr. A often refers to The Universal Ring of Wisdom. When I questioned him about it, he answered, "According to my continuing instructions since boyhood, wisdom comes to us from the earth's protective magnetic ring which surrounds this globe. Here all wisdom and knowledge are stored. There is nothing new under the sun, as I understand it. It's simply a matter of being in tune to receive it. The waves from The Ring, coming through my brain, are automatically translated into words, and the same waves coming through to those of other nationalities are translated into the language of the person receiving them.

"This human ray energy has its origin in a portion of the Power of Powers, and this part is composed of our sun, together with the suns of two other solar systems. This was referred to as the Ancient Trinity."

I do not understand how this method works, but neither can I comprehend how a switch, turned on in my living room, can bring live baseball from Japan, soccer from England, Presidential visits to China and Russia, or a walk on the surface of the moon. We are told that these television pictures are instantly transmitted by means of vibrations bounced off manmade satellites, but how many of us can comprehend the principle involved? Mr. A has been compared with a radio station which both sends and receives signals. He simply says that he tunes into the protective ring encircling this planet and storing within it all knowledge since the beginning of time.

A recent article in the factual *U.S. News & World Report* (April 17, 1972) tells about the many "pure science" automated satellites launched by the United States which have "discovered and mapped in detail the highly complex magnetic field around the earth." There is that term "magnetic field" again! Even our top scientists now concede that it exists, but the mystery is how to harness it for the greater good of mankind.

Our forefathers would have told us to stop daydreaming, if we had chattered about the possibility of American men walking on the moon and of picture tubes in our houses. Should we, then, similarly dismiss as idle chatter the seemingly miraculous wonders performed by this man who automatically comprehends the so-called mysteries of the universe and who was apparently born to heal?